THE BEST PUB JOKE BOOK Ever! 5

ANIMAL JOKES • SILLY SAYINGS • MEN VS. WOMEN JOKES • NAUGHTY JOKES

THIS IS A CARLTON BOOK

This edition published by Carlton Books Limited 2005
20 Mortimer Street
London W1T 3JW

A CIP catalogue record for this book is available from the British Library.

ISBN 1 84442 564 9

Set by e-type, Liverpool
Printed in Great Britain

THE BEST PUB JOKE BOOK Ever! 5

ANIMAL JOKES • SILLY SAYINGS • MEN VS. WOMEN JOKES • NAUGHTY JOKES

CARLTON BOOKS

Contents

Chapter 1
Animal jokes

DOWN, BOY

What has four legs and one arm?
A happy pit bull terrier.

ANIMAL CUNNING

A wealthy old lady decides to go on a photo safari in Africa. She takes her faithful pet poodle along for company. One day, the poodle starts chasing butterflies and before long the poodle discovers that he is lost. So, wandering about, he notices a leopard heading rapidly in his direction with the obvious intention of having lunch. The poodle thinks, 'OK, I'm in deep trouble now!' Then he noticed some bones on the ground close by, and immediately settles down to chew on the bones with his back to the approaching big cat. Just as the leopard is about to leap, the poodle exclaims loudly, 'Boy, that was one delicious leopard. I wonder if there are any more around here?' Hearing this, the leopard halts his attack in mid-stride, a look of terror comes over him and slinks away into the trees. 'Whew,' says the leopard. 'That was close. That poodle nearly had me.' Meanwhile, a monkey who has been watching the whole scene from a nearby tree figures he can put this knowledge to good use and trade it for protection from the leopard. So off he goes. But the poodle sees him heading after the leopard with great speed, and figures that something must be up. The monkey soon catches up with the leopard, spills the beans and strikes a deal for himself with the leopard. The leopard is furious at being made a fool of and says, 'Here, monkey; hop on my back and see what's going to happen to that conniving canine.' Now the poodle sees the leopard coming with the monkey on his back, and thinks, 'What am I going to do now?' But instead of running, the poodle sits down with his back to his attackers, pretending he hasn't seen them yet... and just when they get close enough to hear, the poodle says: 'Where's that damn monkey? I sent him off half an hour ago to bring me another leopard!'

FURBALLS

This old lady is sitting in her living room, reflecting upon her long life, alone and cold. Just when she's ready to go upstairs to her lonely bed, she decides to polish an old lamp she's had in her display cabinet for aeons. Wouldn't you know it: a fairy pops out of the lamp and, by way of thanks, grants her three wishes.

'Well, I'd like to be wealthy for a change,' the old lady says.

The fairy waves her wand and stacks of banknotes appear on the lace-covered table.

'That's rather jolly,' the old lady says. 'Well, I guess I'd like to be a young and beautiful princess.'

Pouf: here she is, transformed into a stunning young girl of around 25. She swirls around and notices her cat sitting near the electric fire.

'Maybe you could transform him into a handsome prince for me?'

With a blinding flash of light, the cat is changed into the most gorgeous-looking stud the old lady has ever seen.

The cat stretches erotically, then walks to her and says: 'Guess you regret having me neutered now, hey?'

VORACIOUS APPETITES

A woman is having fun with her lover in the bedroom when suddenly she hears a car stop in the driveway. She jumps out of bed and rushes to the window.

'It's my husband! Quick! Hide in the bathroom!'

The lover scrambles to the bathroom just in time. The husband enters the bedroom and finds his wife lying on the bed.

'What are you doing on the bed with no clothes on?' he asks.

'I thought you might get back from work early, so I thought… you know…' she purrs.

The husband is quite pleasantly surprised. 'I'll just nip into the bathroom. Back in a jiffy.'

Before his wife has the time to react, he's in the bathroom, where the lover is naked, clapping his hands in the air.

'Who are you?' the husband asks, utterly flabbergasted.

'I'm from the pest control company,' he replies, 'taking care of this moth problem your wife phoned us about.'

'But… you have no clothes on!'

The guys looks at him with round eyes, turns around and pats himself and says with a knowing half-smile: 'Quick little buggers, aren't they?'

GEE UP

It is a very important race for this jockey and he's unlucky enough to have to ride a new horse he's never ridden before.

'Don't worry about it,' the trainer tells him. 'He's very good, honest. He's got a little quirk, though: just before you jump, you'll have to shout, 'One, two, three, jump!' and you'll be fine.'

The jockey doesn't have time to voice his disbelief when he and his horse are called to the line. Off they go, and here comes the first fence. The jockey ignores the trainer's advice and the horse goes crashing into the jump, sending the jockey head over heels.

Quickly he remounts and off they go. This time, though, the jockey does some thinking and realises that acting a bit ridiculous is better than losing the race, so when it's time to jump again, he whispers, 'One, two, three, jump!' into the horse's ear… to no avail. The horse goes crashing into the jump and sends him flying again.

Pissed off and bruised, the jockey remounts and this time at the third fence shouts loudly, 'One, two, three, JUMP!' It's a miracle: the horse gracefully clears the fence and performs a fantastic jump. It's far too late for the jockey, though, who finishes the race well behind the rest of the field.

Dismounting and leading the horse by the bridle, he

goes to the trainer. 'What's the matter with this damn horse?' he explodes. 'Is he deaf?'

'No, he's not deaf, you idiot: he's blind!' he replies.

INSTRUCTIONS FOR GIVING YOUR CAT A PILL

1. Pick cat up from in front of fireplace. Cradle cat in the crook of your left arm as if you were holding a baby. Position right forefinger and thumb on either side of cat's mouth and gently apply pressure to cheeks while holding pill in right hand. As cat opens mouth, pop pill into mouth. Allow cat to close mouth and swallow.
2. Clean any floor dust from pill and retrieve cat from behind sofa. Cradle cat in left arm and repeat process.
3. Retrieve cat from bedroom and throw soggy pill away. Take new pill from packet, cradle cat in left arm holding rear paws tightly with left hand. Force jaws open and push pill to back of mouth with right forefinger. Hold mouth shut for a count of 10.
4. Retrieve pill from goldfish bowl and cat from top of wardrobe. Call spouse from garden.
5. Kneel on floor with cat wedged firmly between knees, holding front and rear paws. Ignore low growls emitted by cat. Get spouse to hold cat's head firmly with one hand while forcing wooden ruler into mouth. Drop pill down ruler and rub cat's throat vigorously for a minute.
6. Retrieve cat from under the bed, get another pill from

packet. Make note to buy new ruler and repair curtains. Carefully sweep Auntie Althea's shattered collection of china dolls and set to one side for glueing later.

7. Wrap cat in large towel and get spouse to lie on cat with its head just visible from below spouse's armpit. Put pill in end of drinking straw, force cat's mouth open with pencil and blow down drinking straw to propel pill.
8. Mime spouse to hit you on the back to prevent choking. Check label to make sure pill not harmful to humans: drink glass of water to take taste away. Apply band-aid to spouse's forearm and remove blood from carpet with cold water and soap.
9. Retrieve cat from neighbour's roof. Get another pill. Cram cat in cupboard and close door on to neck to leave head showing. Force mouth open with dessert spoon. Flick pill down throat with elastic band.
10. Fetch screwdriver from garage and put door back on hinges. Apply cold compress to cheek and check records for date of last tetanus shot. Throw bloody T-shirt away and fetch new one from bedroom.
11. Ring fire brigade to retrieve cat from tree across the road. Take last pill from packet.
12. Tie cat's front paws to rear paws with garden twine and bind tightly to leg of dining table. Find heavy-duty gardening gloves from shed. Force cat's mouth open with any metallic object resistant enough. Push pill into mouth followed by large gob of catfood. Hold cat vertically by rear legs and pour half a pint of water down throat to wash pill down.
13. Get spouse to drive you to emergency room; sit

quietly while doctor stitches fingers and forearm and removes pill remnants from right eye. Stop by furniture shop on way home to order new table.

14. Arrange for vet to make a house call.

IF ONLY THEY COULD TALK

A puppy comes back from school and is greeting by his adoring mother.

'So, how was school today? Did you have fun?'

'Woof! Woof!'

'Did you enjoy physical education today?'

'Wooooof!'

'What about the foreign language lesson? How did it go?'

'Meow! Meow!'

A CLASSIC

What do you call a deer that's got no eyes, is bleeding and is having sex?

No bloody fucking eye deer.

FACTS OF LIFE

A little girl wants to take Beauty the dog for a walk, so she asks permission from her mother.

'You can't take Beauty for a walk right now: she's in heat,' her mum replies.

'What does that mean?

'Go and ask your dad,' eludes the mother, embarrassed. 'He's in the garage.'

The little girl goes and finds her dad in the garage, busy repairing her bike. She explains that she wants to take Beauty for a walk but that she's in heat. With a sigh and a promise to have a word with her mum, the resourceful dad picks up a rag, dips it in some petrol he has in a jerry-can and daubs the rear end of the dog with it, thinking the smell will deter male dogs from approaching her.

'Here you go,' he tells the little girl. 'You can take Beauty for a walk now, but not too far, OK?'

The girl is off and comes back 20 minutes or so later with no dog.

'Where's Beauty?' asks the dad.

'Oh, she ran out of petrol and another dog's pushing her home now.'

NO SCONES FOR ME, THANKS

What do you call a spider with no legs?

A raisin.

A DOG'S DINNER

It is the third time this month that this guy's been burgled. He's had enough and decides to get a dog to protect his house.

He goes to the dog centre and tells his woes to the trainer.

'Don't worry: I have a dog that will do the trick,' the guy says.

They walk around the compound and the buyer stops by a cage holding a fierce-looking German Shepherd.

'Nah," says the trainer, "I have a better dog than that for you.'

They carry on and pass by another cage. A huge, ominous-looking Great Dane hurls itself at the fencing, barking like mad and covering the guy with spit.

'Wow,' he says taking a step back. 'Now that's what I call an attack dog!'

'Yeah, not bad, but this isn't the dog I had in mind for you.'

So they carry on and arrive at a small cage. There's this innocent-looking dog in there, licking his balls.

'Here you go,' the trainer says.

'What: that? Doesn't seem that dangerous to me!'

'I know he doesn't look the part now, but that's only because he's just been eating a lawyer and he's trying to get the taste out of his mouth.'

STICKY MOMENTS

A scientist is studying frogs in a Brazilian swamp and is quite puzzled. The frog population is dwindling, although the males look healthy enough. After a week of research, he realises there's something in the water that prevents the frogs from staying together long enough to copulate, as if it was too oily or something. He goes back to his camp and, with his assistant, concocts some potion which he puts in a large aquarium, together with water samples from the swamp. They're at it for another week before stumbling upon the right combination: some algae extract, chemicals of some sort and a pinch of salt. As they watch the frogs happily reproducing, the scientist remarks: 'Who would have guessed? They need monosodium glue to mate.'

SCROTAL RECALL

A tourist in Egypt is sipping a cocktail and watching a camel tethered to a post. An Arab man comes up to him and asks: 'Do you want to bet I can make this camel jump three metres into the air?'

The bet is made. The Arab grabs a couple of bricks, slowly approaches the unsuspecting camel from the rear and puts the bricks between the camel's legs. There is a loud clap and the camel jumps into the air.

Money changes hands. The Arab then says: 'Do you think I can make this animal say Yes?'

'No way: camels are just too dumb,' the tourist says.

The Arab man picks up the bricks again, walks up to the camel and whispers: 'Do you remember me?'

And the camel nods his head…

MAKES SENSE

What animal goes: Oooooo?

A cow with no lips.

ONE FOR YOU INTELLECTUALS

A tiny snail has had enough of people poking fun at him. He goes to the car dealer and says: 'I want to buy a car. I want the kind of car all the girls will look at when I drive past.'

The dealer is happy to oblige and sells him a flame-red convertible.

'I want to have a big S painted on the bonnet: an S as in snail, so that everybody knows who's driving,' is the little snail's next request.

And sure enough, when he's driving his car around town, every girl turns their head and marvels: 'Did you see that S car go?'

SMALL BUT DEADLY

A guy walks into a bar and says: 'Whose is this Rottweiler my poodle just killed?'

'What? Your poodle killed my Rottweiler? Get out of here!'

'Oh, yes, he did,' confirms the guy. 'He's stuck inside your dog's throat.'

THE OBLIGATORY ELEPHANT'S DICK JOKE

An elephant and a mouse are walking in the forest one day when the elephant falls into a hole. The hole is very, very deep and, try as he might, the elephant can't get out of it. The mouse can't really help because she's so small, but she comes up with an idea.

'Hold on!' she says to the elephant. 'I'll be back in no time and rescue you.'

A few minutes later, the mouse comes back driving a Porsche. She ties a rope to the car and pulls the elephant out of the hole. The elephant is very impressed and grateful.

They carry on walking and, wouldn't you know it, it's the mouse's turn to fall into a hole from which she can't get out. The elephant can't really grab her and is afraid he might hurt her if he's not careful, so he lets his penis hang into the hole and tells the mouse to hold on to it and climb out. Which she does.

Moral: If your dick is big enough, you don't need a Porsche.

DIRTY BIRDY

A guy buys a parrot from a specialist shop and brings it home. As soon as the bird is installed on its perch, he starts swearing obscenely.

'Stop that!' exclaims the owner, shaking the perch.

This seems to rattle the bird and it starts swearing louder than before, screaming stuff to make a veteran sailor blanch.

'I said stop that!' screams the guy, grabbing the offensive bird and shaking it about.

That doesn't do any good, as the parrot, after clearing its throat for a while, launches another verbal attack vile enough to petrify a professional streetwalker.

Exasperated, the guy grabs the bird and forces it into an empty kitchen cabinet. The bird starts getting irritated now and scratches at the wooden door, screeching like a drunken banshee.

'That does it,' the guy mutters and locks the parrot in the freezer. He can hear a commotion for a while, then all sound stops. The silence is deafening. After a few minutes, there is a knock at the door of the freezer.

'Sir, I humbly apologise for my rude behaviour,' the parrot says to an astonished owner. 'I realise my language was out of order and that you are a man of taste.' The bird hops back on its perch and, bobbing on one leg, asks in a small, afraid voice: 'By the way, what did the chicken do to you?'

BAD DOG

A man is having a nap in a deckchair in the garden when a scraping sound wakes him up. In horror, he sees that his dog is dragging a dead rabbit. and not just any old dead rabbit: the neighbour's daughter's rabbit, a rabbit she's loved since she was a toddler.

He quickly shoos the dog away and picks up the dead rabbit. 'Maybe if I clean it up a bit I can put it back in its cage and no one will say anything. They'll think he died there,' he reasons, in his half-awake state. He goes into the garage and cleans up the dead rabbit as well as he can, removing soil from the fur and checking that there aren't any tooth marks on it. He then sneaks into the neighbour's garden and carefully places the animal back in its cage. When all this is done, he returns to his deckchair, waiting for the neighbours to come back from shopping.

After an hour or so, he hears the neighbour's car pulling into the drive. So far so good: maybe his ruse has worked and no one will think his dog killed the rabbit.

Then, suddenly, a piercing cry: 'Daddy!'

'Here we go,' he thinks, saddened by the anguish he can hear in the neighbour's daughter's cry.

'I can't believe it,' he hears the neighbour's dad exclaim in outrage. 'What kind of a sick weirdo would dig up a little girl's dead rabbit and put it back in its cage?'

IT'S THAT CHICKEN AGAIN

Here are a few answers to the age-old question, 'Why did the chicken cross the road?'

Primary school teacher: To get to the other side.
Richard Nixon: The chicken did not cross the road.
Bill Gates: Microsoft has just released a security update to its chicken software that prevents it from behaving in

a way that might be detrimental to your equipment, such as crossing roads.

Homer Simpson: Mmmm … Chicken …

Ronald Reagan: I forgot.

Jack Nicholson: 'cause it f***g wanted to, that's why the f***g chicken crossed the f***g road.

George W Bush: American people will defend the God-given right of chickens to cross whatever road they wish to cross and to live in a chicken world free of chicken-specific terror.

MAKES SENSE IF YOU THINK ABOUT IT

Why are cows always depressed after being milked?

Well, if someone was to wake you up at five in the morning, rub your boobs for a couple of hours and didn't screw you afterwards, you'd feel depressed too!

WISE WORDS INDEED

There was a goose who decided one day not to fly south for the winter. However, the weather soon turned too harsh for the goose to remain where she was and she reluctantly decided to migrate after all. Unfortunately, she was now caught in a snowstorm and, despite her best efforts, got too cold and tired to carry on flying. She fell down and crashed in a barn. Delirious and half-frozen, she saw this huge animal hovering over her and thought it was the end. It was, in fact, a cow, who proceeded to shit copiously on the goose. The warmth of the manure revived the bird and, in thanks, she started to sing for the cow. A fox, hearing the song, came to investigate and soon found the goose. The fox cleaned away the manure and slaughtered the goose.

The moral of the story: People who shit on you are not necessarily your enemies. People who get you out of the shit are not necessarily your friends. If you're warm and happy living in a pile of shit, keep you damn mouth closed.

STRANGE BREW

What do you get if you cross a hyena and an Oxo cube?

A laughing stock.

UP BEFORE THE BEAK

There was this woman who wanted to change her life. She'd tried everything to attract her husband's attention and praise, but he'd always shrugged her off and laughed at her. This had been going on for too long: she needed a change. She needed to dazzle her husband and have him admire her in some way, like he said he did ten years ago before turning into a couch potato, completely uninterested in whatever she did.

All this she explained to the pet shop owner, who replied: 'I understand. You need something unusual, something unique, something that will impress your man. I have what you need.'

He led her to the back of the store where a strange-looking bird was standing forlornly on a wooden perch. The bird was half green, half yellow, had webbed feet and an enormous beak.

'He doesn't look like much but, believe me, this is an

extraordinary bird,' the owner continued. He then addressed the bird this way: 'Goony bird! The shelf!'

As if voice-activated, the bird woke up from its torpor and dashed to the nearest shelf, smashing it to pieces with a few blows of its incredibly powerful beak. Once this was done, it returned to its perch and stood there just as before.

'This is incredible,' the wife exclaimed. 'I'm sure my husband would like it very much: it would be very useful to get rid of all the junk he's got piled up in the shed.'

'All you have to do,' the shopkeeper then explained, 'is to say "Goony Bird" and whatever you want it to smash to pieces.'

Delighted, the woman took the bird home. To test the new pet, she took it to the shed and said: 'Goony Bird! The old table!' Instantly the bird flew to the old, dilapidated table and proceeded to reduce it to a neat pile of splinters in a moment. The woman was over the moon. 'If that doesn't impress him, nothing will,' she thought with a smile.

Holding the bird on its perch, she entered the house and came into the living room, where her husband was busy drinking beer and watching an inane program on TV.

'Darling! Look what I got for you! A Goony Bird!'

The husband, never taking his eyes from the screen, smirked: 'Goony Bird? My ass!'

SUPERSTUD

A couple are visiting a country fair where prize animals are being shown.

'This bull here has coupled 52 times this year,' announces one farmer.

'Fifty-two times?' the wife says, 'that's once a week. You could learn from such a bull.'

The husband doesn't look too pleased by the remark, but says nothing.

The show carries on and they hear that the next bull presented has coupled 104 times this year.

'That's *twice* a week,' exclaims the wife. 'You could take lessons from this bull.' The man grinds his teeth but, once again, prefers to remain silent.

The next bull is shown around and this time its owner says that his bull has been busy 365 times this year.

'Every day!' wonders the woman. 'Wow! You should take an example from that bull!'

'Yeah,' answers the husband, exasperated. 'He did it once every day. But not with the same cow.'

IF THAT'S WHAT IT TAKES...

On a cold day, a man goes down to the frozen lake, cuts a hole in the ice and drops in his fishing line. He waits and waits and nothing bites. Along comes a young boy who cuts a hole in the ice, puts a worm at the end of his fishing line and has a go. After a minute or two, a large fish bites the end of his line and the boy has to struggle to get it out of the water. This goes on for a few fish, until the frustrated man throws his fishing rod down on the ice and walks up to the boy.

'How do you do it?' he asks. 'Two hours freezing my ass off without a nibble and here you come, see... twelve trout in half an hour.'

'Roo Raff Too Geep Fe Rums Rom,' the boy replies.

'Hey? What are you saying? Can't hear a word you say.'

'Roo Raff Too GEEP Fe RUMs ROM,'

The man shakes his head. 'You'll have to speak more clearly, boy, I can't make out a word you're saying.'

The boy then takes out a handful of worms from his mouth.

'You have to keep the worms warm,' he enunciates clearly in an exasperated tone.

THE OLD ONES ARE THE BEST ONES

Two flies are playing football in a saucer. One says to the other: 'We've got to practice; we're in the cup next week.'

PUN FUN

Two dumb guys are standing on a cliff. One of them has a row of budgies attached to his arms; the other has a line of parrots. They both stretch out their arms together and jump.

A day later, in hospital, the first guy tells the second: 'Well, I can't say I think much of this budgie-jumping craze.'

'Yeah: and I won't go paragliding again ever.'

SIZE MATTERS

It is the Flood and Noah has managed to secure a pair of each animal on his ark. Before they go off, though, he gathers all the animals on the deck and says: 'We don't have a lot of room here on this ark, so I am sure you'll understand that we can't allow any sex taking place. I want all the males to come up and hand their pecker to my sons, who will give you a receipt. When the Flood is over, you'll get your pecker back on presentation of the receipt and all will be well.'

This decision is not very popular, but the animals understand that Noah's under a lot of pressure, so they comply.

The situation is particularly strenuous for the rabbit couple. Every day, Mr Rabbit asks his wife to climb on his shoulders to check if there's any land. Every day Mrs Rabbit says that, no, the earth is still covered in water, to which news Mr Rabbit reacts with a nasty oath.

After a week at sea, Mrs Rabbit tells her husband: 'Come on! It's no big deal. I promise we'll have a big party when we land and we'll shag for a week. Don't get too excited.'

'It's not that,' Mr Rabbit replies disconsolately. 'It's just that I've got the donkey's receipt!'

THAT'S HANDY

New breeds of dogs:

Crossing a Collie and a Lhasa Apso will give a Collapso (handy to take with you on travels).

Crossing a Malamute and a Pointer will give a Moot Point, which is... well... it doesn't really matter.

Crossing a Labrador Retriever and a Curly-Coated Retriever will give a Lab Coat Retriever (handy for absent-minded scientists).

Crossing a Newfoundland and a Basset Hound will give a

Newfound Asset Hound (quite prized by financial advisors).

Crossing a Lhasa Apso and a Pekingese will give a Peekasso (a Cubist dog for art-lovers).

Crossing a Collie and a Malamute will give a Commute, a dog that will follow you to work.

THEY'VE GOT TO LEARN

A blind man was waiting at the zebra crossing when his guide dog started peeing on his leg. Unfazed, the blind man reached into his pocket and took out a dog biscuit to give to the dog.

A pedestrian waiting with him on the pavement witnessed the incident, approached the blind man and said: 'This is very decent of you. You're a very tolerant person, after what the dog did to you.'

'Not really,' replies the blind man. 'I'm just checking where his mouth is so I can kick him in the balls.'

SCIENCE HAS THE ANSWER

It is a well-known fact that if you drop a piece of toast, it will always land buttered side on the floor.

It is also a well known fact that if you throw a cat in the air, it will always land on its paws.

Consequently, if one was to strap a piece of toast, butter-side up, to the back of a cat and throw the cat high in the air, one would have a perpetually hovering cat, according to the two laws described earlier.

IF MUSIC BE THE FOOD OF LOVE

A guy enters a Scottish bar with an octopus under his arm. He orders a pint and bets that his pet can play any instrument they can think of. Fortunately, there is a guy in the bar with a guitar. £10 is bet and the octopus picks up the guitar and starts playing. The experiment carries on and the guy is getting rich by having his octopus play a trumpet, a harmonica and an old piano, when an old geezer turns up with his bagpipes.

The octopus looks at the bagpipes with puzzled eyes and is stopped dead in her tracks. Her owner, concerned for his bets, asks her; 'Don't tell me you can't play that!'

'Play it?' the octopus replies in an excited voice. 'As soon as I figure out how to take his pyjamas off, I'm gonna screw him silly.'

PHELINE FYSICS

It is well known that:

Heat flows from a warmer to a cooler body, except in the case of a cat, in which case all heat flows to the cat.

A cat must lie on the floor in such a position as to obstruct the maximum amount of human foot traffic.

If a cat watches a refrigerator long enough, someone will come along and take out something good to eat.

A cat will always seek, and usually take over, the most comfortable spot in any given room.

A cat's desire to scratch furniture is directly proportional to the cost of the furniture.

The best bit in a human body is the belly.

A cat immersed in milk will displace her own volume, minus the amount of milk consumed.

A cat is composed of one part matter, one part anti-matter and one part It Doesn't Matter.

All fabric attracts cat hair. The amount of cat hair attracted is directly proportional to the darkness of the fabric.

LIKE SOME HORRIBLE NIGHTMARE

A man is sitting watching TV one evening when the bell rings. Surprised, because he wasn't expecting anyone, the guy goes to answer the door and finds himself nose to nose with a six-foot cockroach. The cockroach looks him up and down and, without warning, punches him in the nose.

Utterly flabbergasted, the guy doesn't have time to react and the cockroach is gone before he can retaliate.

Back in the house, nursing his bloody nose, the guy hears the doorbell again. He cautiously opens the door and is confronted by the same cockroach, who kicks him solidly in the bollocks before scampering away, laughing maniacally.

Curled on the sofa, blood dripping from his nose, the guy is feeling sorry for himself and is just about to get a swig from a now-warm can of beer when the doorbell rings again. Grabbing a walking stick, the guy pugnaciously swings the door open, only to have the same cockroach fire at him with a pepper-spray gun. While he's on the floor in tears, the cockroach smacks him with a baseball bat and drives both his elbows into each of the guy's kidneys before running off howling.

Crawling back into the living room, the poor guy calls the hospital. The ambulance crew turns up a few minutes later and he explains to them what happened, what with the six-foot cockroach and the baseball bat and the pepper spray and all. The paramedic only nods in sympathy and says: 'Yeah, we know. There's a nasty bug going around.'

VENISON PERIL

This hunter has been chasing a deer for a whole day and comes back home with his prize, quite happy with himself. He decides to clean it and dress it so that he can cook it the following day.

There's a strange aroma in the kitchen the following day, one the kids can't really place. It's strong and pungent and a bit meaty. Nonetheless, whatever's being cooked is placed on the table for the family to eat. Overcome with curiosity and quite fussy about what he eats, the little boy asks his dad: 'What are we eating today, dad?'

The dad smiles and says: 'Well, let's say it's something your mum calls me sometimes.'

The daughter looks at her brother in alarm.

'Don't eat it! It's an asshole!'

HAVE YOU HERD?

The premise is you have two cows. Here is what you do with them if you are:

A Christian:
You give one of the cows to your neighbour out of love but tell them you'll take it back if they milk it on a Sunday.

A Socialist:
The government takes one of them and gives it to your neighbour.

A New Labourite:
You have two cows but your neighbour has none. You feel guilty and promise equality for all the people in the country. You decide that the two cows need to be privatised to maximise milk output. The companies that milk the cows rake in a lot of money: then the cows die and they go bankrupt. You blame the Tories.

A Communist:
The army seizes both cows and provides you with milk.

A Fascist:
Young boys in brown uniforms carrying guns seize the cows. The government then sells you the milk if you can show your family history going back 20 years.

A Capitalist:
You sell one of your cows, buy a bull and soon get a herd.

A Bureaucrat:
A committee decides you have too many cows and takes them away. Another committee decides to kill one of the

cows, while yet another decides to milk the other cow, then wait for the proper directive while the milk goes off.

A Corporation:
You sell one cow for profit and genetically enhance the other cow to produce the milk of three cows. The cow gets sick and dies, so you water the milk down and sell it at the same price while playing down the health risks of genetically contaminated milk.

A Frenchman:
You go on strike because you want three cows. The government gives you three cows and you go on holiday.

A Japanese:
You study the cows and redesign them so that they are one-fifth of the size of an ordinary cow and produce ten times as much milk.

A German:
You redesign your cows so that they milk themselves, and eat one every week. You make schnapps out of the cows' urine as a by-product.

An American:
You have two cows and your neighbour has none. So what?

An Italian:
You don't know where the cows are. You go to lunch.

A Swiss:
You have 5,000 cows, none of which belongs to you and you don't really want to know who they belong to anyway. You charge for storing them for others and buy a small European country.

OOH, THOSE DUCKS!

Three ducks are brought into a police station.

'What's your name?' the desk sergeant asks the first duck.

'Quack.'

'And what were you taken in for?'

'I was blowing bubbles in the pond.'

'Man, this is disgusting! You can't do that; it's against the law! You'll have to pay me a fine, my dear sir.'

The duck agrees to pay the fine and leaves.

'So, what's your name?' the policeman asks the second duck.

'My name is Quack Quack.'

'I see,' the policeman scribbles down the name on a form. 'And what were you arrested for?'

'I was blowing bubbles in the pond.'

'You too? What's the matter with you ducks? Don't you know it's illegal to blow bubbles in the pond? Same fine as your friend!'

The second duck agrees to pay the fine and leaves. The third duck approaches the counter.

'Let me guess. Your name is Quack Quack Quack, right?'

'No: my name is Bubbles.'

LIFE EXPLAINED

On the first day God created the cow. God said, 'You must go to the fields with the farmer all day long and suffer under the sun, have calves and give milk to support the farmer. I will give you a lifespan of 60 years.' The cow said, 'That's a kind of a tough life you want me to live for

60 years. Let me have 20 years and I'll give back the other 40.' And God agreed.

On the second day, God created the dog. God said, 'Sit all day by the door of your house and bark at anyone who comes in or walks past. I will give you a lifespan of 20 years.' The dog said, 'That's too long to be barking. Give me ten years and I'll give back the other ten.' So God agreed (sigh).

On the third day God created the monkey. God said, 'Entertain people, do monkey tricks, make them laugh. I'll give you a 20-year lifespan.' The monkey said, 'How boring: monkey tricks for 20 years? I don't think so. Dog gave you back ten, so that's what I'll do too, OK?' And God agreed again.

On the fourth day God created man. God said, 'Eat, sleep, play, have fun and enjoy life. Do nothing; just enjoy. I'll give you 20 years.' Man said, 'What? Only 20 years? No way, man. Tell you what: I'll take my 20, and the 40 Cow gave back, and the ten Dog gave back and the ten Monkey gave back. That makes 80, OK?' 'OK,' said God. 'You've got a deal.'

So that's why for the first 20 years we eat, sleep, play, enjoy life, and have fun; for the next 40 years we slave in the sun to support our family; for the next ten years we do monkey tricks to entertain our grandchildren; and for the last ten years we sit in front of the house and bark at everybody. Life explained.

Chapter 2
Bar jokes

STRINGING HIM ALONG

A piece of string enters the bar with a few friends and orders a beer. The bartender looks at him and says: 'Sorry mate, we don't serve string here.'

The piece of string, hurt, makes a face and goes to sit, empty-handed, at a table.

A few minutes later, goaded by his friends, the piece of string tries his chance again.

'I told you before, mate: we don't serve string here,' is the barman's answer to his plea for a beer.

The piece of string goes back to his table, now quite thoroughly thirsty. He thinks for some time and comes up with a plan. He messes up the top of his hair, ties himself into a loose loop and goes back to the bar.

'Could I have a beer, please?' he asked innocently.

'Hey, aren't you a bit of string?' the barman asks suspiciously.

'Nope: I'm a frayed knot.'

TWO OF A KIND

A man walked into a Melbourne bar and ordered a pint of the dark liquid. 'Excuse me,' said the only other drinker. 'Is that an Irish accent I detect?' 'It is, sir: Dublin, to be exact.'

'Bless my soul,' said the first. 'I'm a Dublin man meself: Ballymun, to be precise.'

'Bedad, aren't I from Ballymun meself? Carberry Street, in actual fact,' remarked the second. 'Carberry Street is where I was born and raised meself, and St Joseph's was me parish church, Father Dunne the parish priest.'

'Didn't I go to nine o'clock mass every Sunday at St Joseph's? What an amazingly small world. Did you go to St Joseph's School?'

'I did. I was in Miss Slattery's class.'

'God in heaven. So was I.'

Just then the phone rang and the Aussie barman picked it up and, in answer to a question, said, 'Not too busy at the moment. In fact, there's just the Murphy twins here.'

DRINK AUSTRALIAN, THINK AUSTRALIAN

An Australian guy goes into a bar on a Greek island. Jill, the Australian barmaid, takes his order and can't help but notice his accent. Over the course of the night they talk quite a bit.

At the end of the night, he asks her if she wants to have sex with him. Although she is attracted to him, she declines. He then offers to pay her $200 for the deed. Jill, who is travelling the world and a bit short of funds, agrees.

The next night the guy turns up again and after

showing her plenty of attention throughout the night asks if she will sleep with him again for $200. She figures 'In for a penny, in for a pound', and as it was pleasurable the previous night, she agrees.

This goes on for five nights. On the sixth night the guy comes back into the bar. However, this night he orders a beer and just goes and sits in the corner.

Jill is disappointed, and thinks that maybe she should pay him a bit more attention, so she goes over and sits next to him. She asks him where in Australia is he from, and he tells her Melbourne.

'So am I', she says. 'What suburb in Melbourne?'

'Glen Iris', he says.

'That's amazing!' she says, 'So am I. What street?'

'Cameo Street', he says.

'This is unbelievable!' she says. 'What number?'

'Number 20', he replies and she is astonished.

'You're not going to believe this', she says, 'I'm from number 22 and my parents still live there!'

'I know,' he says. 'Your father gave me $1,000 to give you!'

BLONDES HAVE MORE FUNDS

A guy is sitting quietly in a bar, sipping his drink, minding his own business, when a flamboyant blonde comes in and sits right next to him. She orders a drink and it becomes quickly obvious that she's becoming bored fast.

She turns around on her stool and looks at the guy with smouldering eyes.

'I'll screw you anywhere, any time – my place, your place, it doesn't matter,' she whispers huskily.

'Wow!' the guy exclaims. 'What law company do you work for?'

LE MALLARD IMAGINAIRE

A circus director goes into a bar and is surprised to see everybody gathered around a table in the centre of the bar. He elbows his way in and, to his surprise, he finds himself face to face with a duck dancing on a little pot. 'This is great,' he thinks. 'That's one of the best acts I've ever seen.'

He finds out who the owner of the duck is and tries to make a deal. A few minutes of haggling later, he parts with £5,000 and gets both the duck and the pot it's dancing on.

A few days pass and the circus director is back in the bar, seeking the ex-owner out.

'What's that all about?' he rages. 'Your duck hasn't danced for me in three days! I want my money back!'

'Hold on a minute, matey,' the guy replies. 'You say the duck hasn't been dancing at all?'

'That's right!'

'Well, did you remember to light the candle under the pot?'

A WIFE SENTENCE

A seriously drunk guy walks into a bar and orders a drink. He looks around and, after staring for some time at the only woman seated at the bar a few seats away from him, walks over to her and kisses her. Outraged, she jumps up and slaps him full in the face in speechless anger.

The guy puts his hand to his face with wide eyes. 'I'm

sorry. I thought you were my wife. You look exactly like her', he apologises to her.

'Don't give me that bullshit: you're too drunk to recognise your own mother!' she screams.

'Funny,' he muses, scratching his nose in wonder. 'You even sound exactly like her too.'

WHERE'S THIS PLACE AGAIN?

Three blokes are in a pub. It's not a very nice pub: the wallpaper is crap, the seats are uncomfortable and there's no real ale.

'I know a place in Manchester,' sighs the first bloke, 'where you pay for the first beer, you pay for the second and the guv'nor buys you the next.'

'Yeah, there's a place like that in London,' the second guy says. 'The Horse and Pony in Hackney. You buy the first three beers and the landlord buys you the fourth and you get a free pork pie too.'

'I know a place in Birmingham,' the last one says, 'where your first drink is paid for you, the second drink is paid for you, your third drink is paid for you, then you go upstairs and shag all night for free.'

The others are astonished. 'Really? Did it really happen to you?'

'Nah,' says the guy sadly. 'It did happen to my sister, though.'

PARTICLE PHYSICS FOR BEGINNERS

A neutron walks into a bar.

'I'd like a beer', he says.

The bartender promptly serves up a beer.

'How much do I owe you?' asks the neutron.

'For you?' replies the bartender, 'no charge'.

WHY THIS ONE DIDN'T MAKE IT INTO OTHELLO, I'LL NEVER KNOW

William Shakespeare goes into an alehouse in Stratford-upon-Avon and says: 'Good morrow, dear fellow. Would'st thou furnish me with a flagon of thy fine ale, a quaff of which will quench my fierce thirst?'

'Get thou hence: I'll serve thee not!'

'Prithee, wherefore not, good master?'

'I like not the look of thee. Thou art Bard.'

HARSH REALITY

A poor man and woman were sitting on a battered sofa in their living room.

'I'm going down the pub for a bit, so put your coat on', the man said after a while.

'Oh, sweetie, are you taking me out?' the woman replied, flushing with pleasure.

'Nah; I'm turning the heat off.'

IT COULD HAPPEN TO YOU

A man has spent two days in the desert and is now thoroughly parched. On the evening of the third day, he sees a building in the distance. He stumbles along, choking on sand, for another hour and gets to a kind of shop.

'Please, a drink ...' he whispers to the man at the door.

'I'm sorry,' the man says. 'I only sell ties. Can't help you there.'

The thirsty guy begs and implores, to no avail: there is no drink to be had.

He plods on and, on the evening of the third day, he sees a building in the distance. He gathers his last bit of energy and crawls towards the lights. Miracle! Here, in the desert, is a bar! He staggers to the bouncer at the door and croaks: 'Mercy … a drink, please …'

'Sorry, mate,' the bouncer says, 'can't let you in without a tie'.

BLIND LOGIC

A man walks into a bar with his dog.

'Hold on. You can't bring that dog in here!' forbids the barman.

The guy, without missing a beat, says: 'This is my guide dog.'

'Oh, man,' the bartender says, 'I'm sorry. Here: the first one's on me.'

The man takes his drink and goes to a table near the door.

Another guy walks into the bar with a chihuahua. The first guy sees him, stops him and says: 'You can't bring that dog in here unless you tell him it's a guide dog.'

The second man gratefully thanks the first man and continues to the bar. He asks for a drink. The bartender says: 'Hey, you can't bring that dog in here!'

The second man replies 'This is my seeing-eye dog.'

The bartender says, 'No, I don't think so. Since when do they have chihuahuas as guide dogs?'

The man pauses for half a second and replies 'What? They gave me a chihuahua?'

WOULDN'T YOU BE?

A man in a bar sees a friend of his sitting and drinking by himself, looking very down.

'Hey, mate: you look terrible. What's the problem?' he asks him.

'My mother died in August,' his friend replies, 'and left me £25,000.'

'Gee, that's tough.'

'Then in September,' the friend continues, 'my father died, leaving me £90,000.'

'Wow. Two parents gone in two months: no wonder you're depressed.'

'And last month my aunt died and left me £15,000.'

'Three close family members lost in three months? How sad.'

'Then this month,' finishes the friend, 'absolutely nothing!'

GET SHORTY

A guy enters a bar and sits down in silence. After a while, the bartender approaches him and asks: "What'll you have?'

'A scotch, please.'

The bartender hands him the drink and says: 'That'll be £3.'

'What are you talking about? I don't owe you anything for this,' the customer replies with a thin smile.

A lawyer, sitting nearby and overhearing the conversation, says to the bartender: 'You know, he's got you there. In the original offer, which constitutes a binding contract upon acceptance, there was no stipulation of remuneration.'

The bartender is not impressed at all. 'OK, you beat me for a drink. But don't ever let me catch you in here again,' he says in a grumpy tone and walks off to serve another customer.

The next day, the same guy walks into the bar.

'What the hell are you doing in here? I can't believe you've got the audacity to come back!'

The guy says, 'What are you talking about? I've never been here in my life!'

The bartender scratches his head and replies, 'I'm very sorry, but this is uncanny. You must have a double.'

'Thank you very much, my good man. Make it a scotch,' the guy replies with a smile.

PAINFULLY HONEST

John and Jessica are on their way home from the bar one night when John gets pulled over by the police.

'Good evening, Sir,' says the officer. 'It appears that your back light doesn't work.'

'I'm very sorry, officer; I didn't realise it was out. I'll get it fixed right away,' John says with a contrite smile.

Just then, Jessica says, 'I knew this would happen; I told you two days ago to get that light fixed.'

The officer squints sternly at John and asks to see the car's papers. After having examined the papers thoroughly, the policeman says: 'Sir, your MoT has expired.'

John apologises nervously and says he didn't realise it had expired and he'll take care of it first thing in the morning.

Just then Jessica says: 'I told you a week ago that the MoT was due. I even asked you if you wanted to get it booked with a garage but you never answered.'

John grinds his teeth, quite upset with his wife contradicting him in front of the officer.

'Jessica, shut your mouth!' he says to her between clenched teeth.

The officer then leans over towards Jessica and asks, 'Does your husband always talk to you like that?'

'Oh, no: only when he's drunk.' Jessica replies.

THE BEER PRAYER

Our lager,
Which art in barrels,
Hollowed be thy drink.
I will be drunk,
At home as in the tavern.
Give us this day our foamy head,
And forgive us our spillages,
As we forgive those who spill against us.
And lead us not into incarceration,
But deliver us from hangovers.
For thine is the beer, the bitter and the lager
Forever and ever,
Barmen.

ONE FOR THE FEMINISTS

Yesterday, scientists revealed that beer contains small traces of female hormones.

To prove their theory, they fed 100 men 12 pints of beer and observed that 100 per cent of them started talking nonsense and couldn't drive.

CHILDREN OF THE NIGHT

Three vampires walk into a vampire bar and sit at the counter. The waitress comes up to them and asks them what they'd like to drink.

'I'd like a glass of blood,' says the first vampire.

The waitress acquiesces and serves him a glass of foaming, warm blood.

'I'd like a glass of O positive, please,' says the second guy.

The waitress complies and hands him a tankard of O positive, nicely coagulated.

'What about you?' she asks the last guy.

'Er… I'd like a mug of hot water, please.'

The waitress gasps and her eyes widen. The other customers turn around and look at the last guy, showing expectant pointed teeth, ready to tear him apart. The whole bar is silent apart from the fluttering of bat wings.

The guy then takes a used Tampax out of his pocket and says; 'Yeah: I feel like a herbal tea.'

WE'VE ALL BEEN THERE

A drunken man gets on the bus late one night outside the pub, staggers up the aisle and sits next to an elderly woman.

She looks the man up and down and says in a very

reproving tone: 'I've got news for you. You're going straight to hell!'

'Man, I'm on the wrong bus!' shouts the man, jumping up out of his seat.

TILL DEATH...

A guy walks into a bar and orders a stiff drink. Then he asks for another. After a couple more drinks, the bartender gets worried.

'What's the matter with you?' the bartender asks.

'My wife and I got into a fight,' explains the guy 'and now she hasn't been talking to me for a whole month.'

The bartender thinks about this for a while and then asks him: 'But isn't it a good thing that she isn't talking to you?'

'Yeah, except tonight's the last night,' he replies forlornly.

HOW DRUNK ARE YOU?

Official drinking test.

Here is a set of five multiple-choice questions. Answer as truthfully as you can, note your answers down if you are able and check the result with the chart at the end. This will help you determine how drunk you really are compared to how drunk you think you are.

1. Think about the girl sitting next to you. In your mind, is she

(a) the most beautiful woman you've ever met
(b) a beautiful woman: quite sexy, too
(c) attractive
(d) ugly as sin?

2. Think about your job. In your mind, is it:
(a) the best job on the planet
(b) a good job
(c) a decent job
(d) the most annoying job ever?

3. Try walking. What happened? Did you
(a) find it impossible to stand up
(b) fall after standing up
(c) walk 50 feet before falling flat on your face
(d) walk 500 yards without falling?

4. How did you get to the bar? I got here in
(a) my brand-new chauffeur-driven limo
(b) a brand-new car
(c) a used car
(d) I don't remember?

5. What do you think of your strength? I am
(a) invincible
(b) stronger than anyone in the bar
(c) as strong as the average man
(d) a weak and pathetic joke of a man?

Scoring:
For every question answered with an A, add ten points.
For every question answered with a B, add five points.
For every question answered with a C, do not change the score.
For every question answered with a D, subtract five points.
For every question answered with an E, add one hundred points.

Results

51 to 135

Congratulations. You are quite thoroughly drunk. Somewhere along this test you have even managed to answer E, when there wasn't an E option available. That requires some doing. You're way beyond the normal drunk. The state you're in probably doesn't have a name yet. You are feeling like a Shaolin martial arts master, ready to take on the whole of the bar, including the bouncers, before driving off with the hot bird next to you for a night of crazy sex and champagne in the stretch limo you won on the Lottery. None of this is true, but you're going to go ahead and do it anyway. You've just spent 20 minutes arguing about the merits of Rochester City Football Club with a single-service packet of ketchup and you lost. There is more alcohol in your veins than there are red cells left. You can't pronounce words with more than one syllable. In fact, you can't pronounce words at all. You have just spent your pay packet, plus a sizeable portion of next month's and that of the wife's too, all in one night. Not even the fuzzy knowledge that the state you will be in tomorrow will be the proportional inverse of the one you are in now can stop you from ordering another one. There is no hope for you. Well done.

36 to 50

You've had ten too many beers. If you plan on driving home, make out a will first: that is, if you can even remember your own name (no, it's not Clark Kent). Don't bother trying to stand up; you'll just smack back down again. Just try to crawl your way out of the bar. Tomorrow evening, when you wake up, you'll discover bruises and strange patches of dried stuff all over you and your breath will smell as if a small furry animal died in your mouth during the night. You can probably do better next time, but it will take some doing. Not bad. A worthy effort.

15 to 35

You've had three too many beers. If you drive home tonight, it will probably be the last time for six months. Standing up will probably result in injury but you can still do it, although please don't lean on the bouncer's shoulder and tell him he's your best friend: that'll just irritate him. In your state, you don't want to irritate anybody any more than you already have been for the past three hours with your pointless life story. At present, you're only pathetically drunk: stop before it's too late.

0 to 14

You may want to stop drinking right now. You have had enough beers to remain roughly coherent but that will change if you order another one for the road. You've reach the limit and the barman knows it –as do all your other drinking colleagues. You still have all your clothes on, some money in your pocket to get a cab home and you haven't puked in a flowerpot yet, so spare yourself this indignity and give up now. There will still be bits you won't remember tomorrow, so the night isn't a complete waste.

-25 to 1

Right. You'd better get started otherwise you'll have to listen to your mates' intimate problems for the rest of the evening and learn things that will haunt you for the rest of your life unless you drink enough to obliterate all memories tomorrow morning. Also, think about it: who wants to be the taxi for the night, hey? Surely not you. Chill out. Wrap your tie around your forehead and order a whisky. There. You can do it.

A NORSE, A NORSE, MY KINGDOM FOR A NORSE...

A guy was sitting alone on his train journey to London when a couple of Norwegians entered the carriage. Sven was dressed in a smart business suit while his friend Olf was dressed as a Teddy Boy.

After a little while, Olf stood up and went to the buffet car for a beer. He brought it back to the carriage, opened it and took a swig. He spat it out straight away, swearing loudly in Norwegian.

'What's the matter with him?' asked the guy.

'I apologise', replied Sven. 'Rude Olf the Ted loathes train beer.'

THE START OF A CHRISTMAS TRADITION

One particular Christmas season a long time ago Santa was getting ready for his annual trip, but there were problems everywhere.

Four of his elves fell ill and the trainee elves didn't produce the toys as fast as the regular ones, so Santa was beginning to feel the pressure of being behind schedule.

Then Mrs Claus told Santa that her mum was coming to visit. This stressed Santa even more. When he went to harness the reindeer, he found that three of them were about to give birth and two had jumped the fence and were out, Heaven knows where. More stress.

Then when he began to load the sleigh one of the boards cracked and the toy bag fell to the ground and scattered the toys.

So, frustrated, Santa went into the house for a cup of coffee and a shot of whisky. When he went to the cupboard, he discovered that the elves had hidden the liquor and there was nothing to drink. In his frustration, he accidentally dropped the coffee pot and it broke into hundreds of little pieces all over the kitchen floor.

He went to get the broom and found that mice had eaten the straw it was made from.

Just then the doorbell rang and Santa cursed on his way to the door. He opened the door… and there was a little angel with a great big Christmas tree.

The angel said, very cheerfully, 'Merry Christmas, Santa. Isn't it just a lovely day? I have a beautiful tree for you. Isn't it just a lovely tree? Where would you like me to stick it?'

And thus began the tradition of the little angel on top of the Christmas tree.

HER INDOORS

One night, Joe tells his wife he's heading out to the pub for a drink. His wife starts complaining that he never takes her anywhere any more, that he doesn't show her he loves her like when they first started dating and that he doesn't care. She keeps going for hours and hours. Fed-up and seeing that it's getting late, Joe gives in and agrees to take his wife to the pub. They sit down at a table and Joe gets up and goes to get drinks for himself and the missus.

While he's away, a man walks up to Joe's wife and tells her he wants to turn her upside-down, fill her with beer and drink her dry.

'You sick pervert! Get out of my sight, you bastard! Wait until my husband comes back!' is Joe's wife's quite predictable reaction.

When Joe does return, his wife relates the incident to him and points at the guy's back in the crowd.

'Go and kick his ass!' she demands, outraged and furious.

Joe glances at the offending bloke and says: 'No way, honey. I won't mess with a guy who can drink that much beer'.

IT HAD TO HAPPEN

A dyslexic guy walks into a bra…

THAT STUFF'LL KILL YOU

A man is in the habit of having a shot of whisky every night before he goes to bed. For years this habit has been irritating his wife no end, but she's never managed to persuade him to stop.

Fed-up, she decides to resort to a little object lesson one night. She takes two glasses and fills one up with water, the other with whisky. She then opens his tackle box and picks up a worm.

'Look closely,' she says to her husband and drops the worm in the glass full of water. The worm wriggles a bit, looking bored, but survives. She then repeats the experiment with another worm, which she drops into the glass full of whisky. The worm thrashes a bit, convulses, then dies.

'See?' she asks triumphantly. 'do you understand what will happen if you keep drinking whisky?'

The husband, without missing a beat, replies cheerfully: 'Yes, I see now. If I keep on drinking whisky, I won't get worms!'

ONE OF THOSE DAYS

A man walks into a bar after a long day at work. As he begins relaxing and drinking his beer, he hears a seductive voice purr: 'You've got great hair!'

He looks around but can't see where the voice is coming from, so he goes back to his beer. A minute or so later, he hears the same soft voice again, which says: 'You're a handsome man!' Puzzled, the guy looks around, but still can't see where the voice is coming from. He goes back to his beer, only to hear the voice say: 'Like your shirt!'

The man is so baffled by this that he finally goes up to the barman and asks him what is going on.

'Oh, it's nothing,' the barman answered. 'It's the nuts. They're complimentary.'

HOW SILLY OF ME

A Pommie ends up in a bar in Queensland. No one looks up from their beer when he orders a mint julep. The Pommie sips his drink, quite self-consciously in the presence of all these weatherbeaten, huge and muscular Aussies. After a while, he feels the urge to relieve himself and, in a small voice, asks the barman where the toilets are. As expected, they are outside. So our Pommie surreptitiously leaves the bar through the back exit and walks for a few yards, before coming across two piles of shit. One pile is significantly smaller than the other. He unbuttons his trousers, thinking that at least some customers in this barbaric bar have had the presence of mind to start a new pile when the first one was obviously beginning to be unmanageable.

It is in the weak and undignified crouching position adopted by people the world over when they are having a crap (be they Pommie, Aussie or Chinese) that the barman finds him. With an outraged gasp, the barman seizes the rifle he always goes out with in case he feels the urge to shoot down a kangaroo and shoots right between the Pommie's legs, spraying him with shit.

'What are you doing, you dirty bastard?' he thunders. 'Get out of the Ladies' right now!'

RETURN OF THE PUN KING

A man walks into a bar and orders a pint of beer. He looks around, admiring the room and the decoration and he soon notices that there are big lumps of what looks like meat hanging from the ceiling.

'Er… why have you got all this meat hanging down in your bar?', he asks the barman.

'It's a little bet we're running,' the barman replies. 'If you can jump up and grab a bit of meat in your mouth, then you get all your drinks bought for you. If you fail, then you have to buy a drink for everyone else in the bar. Want to give it a go?'

The man looks at the crowd in the pub and shakes his head.

'No,' he replies, 'the steaks are too high.'

ACID-TONGUED

An obviously intoxicated gentleman staggers into a bar and seats himself at the counter. After being served, he notices a woman sitting a few stools down. He motions the bartender over and says: 'Bartender, I'd like to buy that old douche bag down there a drink.'

Somewhat offended, and seeing that the woman has heard the exchange, the bartender replies: 'Sir, I run a respectable establishment and I don't appreciate you calling my female customers douche bags.'

The man looks ashamed of himself and mutters: 'You're right; that was uncalled for... please allow me to buy her a cocktail.'

'That's better,' says the bartender. 'Ma'am, the gentleman down the bar would like to buy you a drink: what would you like?'

'How nice!' replies the woman sourly, 'I'll have a vinegar and water.'

MAN'S BEST FRIEND

A guy walks into a bar and sees a dog lying in the corner licking his balls. He turns to the bartender and says: 'Boy, I wish I could do that.'

The bartender replies, 'You'd better try petting him first.'

RIGHT BACK AT YA

A guy walks into a bar. The music is quite loud. Nonetheless, he sits down at the counter. He spots a pretty girl at the end of the bar and approaches her.

'Would you like to dance?' he asks her.

She looks him up and down with a disgusted grimace or her face and says: 'I really don't like this song. And even if I did, I wouldn't dance with you.'

Pissed off by this attitude, the guy replies: 'I don't think you heard me correctly. I said your skirt makes your ass look fat.'

GOOD SAVE

A guy is getting bored alone in a bar after a few beers, so he tries his luck with the girl sitting next to him.

'Do you mind if I ask you a personal question?' he said to her, convinced, in his drunken state, that this is a great chat-up line.

'I don't know,' replies the young woman, suspicious. 'It depends how personal it is.'

'Tell me: how many men have you slept with?'

'I'm not going to tell you that!' the woman exclaimed. 'That's my business!'

'Sorry,' blurts the guy, with a wave of his hand. 'I didn't realise you made a living out of it.'

TIME TO CALL IT A DAY

A man walks in through the front door of a bar. He is obviously drunk. He staggers up to the bar, seats himself on a stool and, with a belch, asks the bartender for a drink.

The bartender politely informs the man that it appears he has already had plenty to drink. Consequently, he will not be serving him any more drinks, but he could get a cab called for him.

The drunk is briefly surprised, then softly scoffs, grumbles, climbs down off the barstool and staggers out the front door.

A few minutes later, the same drunk stumbles in the side door of the bar. He wobbles up to the bar and hollers for a drink. The bartender comes over and, still politely – although a bit more firmly – refuses service to the man due to his inebriation. Again, the bartender offers to call a cab for him.

The drunk looks at the bartender for a moment angrily, curses and shows himself out via the side door, all the while grumbling and shaking his head.

A few minutes later, the same drunk bursts in through the back door of the bar. He plops himself up on a bar stool, gathers his wits and belligerently orders a drink.

The bartender comes over and emphatically reminds the man that he is clearly drunk, will be served no drinks and that either a cab or the police will be called immediately.

The surprised drunk looks at the bartender and in hopeless anguish cries 'Man! How many bars do you work at?'

A FOAL AND HIS MONEY

A pony walks into a bar and says 'May I have a drink?'

The barman frowns and says: 'What? I can't hear you. Speak up!'

'May I please have a drink?'

'What? You'll have to speak up!'

'Could I please have a drink?'

'Now, listen: if you don't speak up I won't serve you.'

'I'm sorry: I'm just a little hoarse.'

LOOK AT IT THIS WAY

A guy walks into a bar with a frog on his head.

'Hey, what's that?' asks the bartender.

'I don't know,' replies the frog. 'It started as a wart on my bum and this happened.'

SHORT ARMS, DEEP POCKETS

One night, a drunk comes stumbling into a bar and says to the bartender: 'Drinks for everyone on me, including you, bartender.'

So the bartender follows the guy's orders and when all the drinks have been handed over says: 'That'll be £150, please.'

The drunk admits he has no money. The bartender, incensed, slaps him around and throws him out.

The next night the same drunk comes in again and orders a drink for everyone in the bar, including the bartender. Again the bartender follows his instructions, and once again the drunk says he has no money. The bartender slaps him around a bit harder and throws him out once more.

On the third night, the drunk comes in once again and orders drinks for all except the bartender.

'What; no drink for me?' replies the bartender with heavy sarcasm.

'Oh, no. You get violent when you drink.'

OOPS

Every night after dinner, Harry was in the habit of heading off to the local tavern. He would spend the whole evening there and would come back home very drunk around midnight every night.

His wife, waiting up for him, would go to the door and let him in. Then she would proceed to yell and scream at him, for his constant nights out, his coming home in a drunken state, for longer and longer every year – but Harry carried on.

One day, the wife cracked up and sought counsel from one of her friends. The friend listened to her patiently and then said: 'Why don't you treat him a little differently when he comes home? Instead of shouting at him, why don't you welcome him home with some kind words and a kiss? That might make him change his ways.' The wife thought it over and convinced herself that might be a good idea. In any case, it wouldn't hurt to try.

So that night, after dinner, Harry took off again. About midnight he arrived home in his usual condition. His wife heard him at the door and let Harry in. This time, instead of shouting at him, as she had always done, she took his arm and led him into the living room. She sat him down in an easy chair, put his feet up on a stool and took his shoes off. Then she went behind him and started to cuddle him a little and massage his shoulders. After a little while, she said to him: 'It's pretty late, dear. What about going upstairs to bed now?'

At that, Harry replied, in his inebriated state, 'I guess we might as well. I'll be getting into trouble with the stupid wife when I get home anyway!'

DODGY DOGGY

A guy walks into a bar with a weird dog on a leash: he's stumpy-legged, pink, and doesn't have a tail.

The barman spots him and says, with a greedy look in his eyes: 'I bet my Rottweiler would beat the heck out of your dog, mate.'

A bet of £50 is duly made, but out in the yard the Rottweiler gets mauled to pieces.

A customer, surveying the scene, raises the stakes: he's got a pit-bull that will tear this weird dog to pieces, but the bet has to be £100. Another trip to the yard and, when it's all over, there are bits of pit-bull terrier all over the place.

The customer, dismayed, pays up and says: 'Say, what breed is this dog anyway?'

The owner says, 'Until I cut his tail off and painted him pink, he was the same breed as every other alligator.'

YOU ASKED FOR IT

Two friends are meeting in a bar.

'You're wearing an earring now? I didn't know: it's not really your style and it doesn't look that healthy, either. It's all red and puffy. Is it recent?'

'Er… since my wife found one in the car.'

THAT'S ALL RIGHT, THEN

A newlywed couple enters the bar. One of the groom's old friends, someone he hasn't seen for ages, is there already. They shake hands, clap one another on the back and the husband introduces his wife to his friend. The friend looks surprised but says nothing. The three of them sit down at a table. After a while, having talked about their lives for a while, the two men are quite drunk. The friend has been looking at the wife from time to time, with a puzzled expression. In the end, he can't take it any more and bends over to the young husband and whispers: 'You know, we're friends; we've known each other for a long time, even if we don't see each other very often. Tell me: what do you see in her? I mean: she's fat, she's old, she's nearly bald…'

'No need to whisper,' his friend says with a smile. 'She's deaf.'

WILD WILD WEST

A cowboy is at the bar with a friend.

'You see that guy there at that table: the one with big boots?'

'Er… they all wear big boots.'

'The one who's smoking.'

'Man, they're all smoking.'

'The guy there; the one who's playing poker!'

'Well, they're all playing cards.'

Exasperated, the cowboy takes his gun out and shoots three of the four guys at the table.

'Now do you see the one I mean?'

'Yeah, now I do'

'I hate that guy.'

I'M ON THE TOILET

After a few beers, a guy has to head for the gents'. He sits down and starts his business when he hears another person entering the cubicle next to him.

Then he hears: 'How are you doing?'

The guy is quite shocked and doesn't know what to say. Finally, he says: 'Er… I'm fine, thanks.'

'You're having a good time?'

The guy is embarrassed; he's never found himself in such a situation before.

'Er… yeah, it's all right.'

There is a short silence: then the voice is heard again: 'Listen, I'll call you back in a moment. There's an idiot in the next cubicle who keeps talking to me.'

Chapter 3
Blonde jokes

QUESTIONS, QUESTIONS

A blonde is sitting alone in a bar, getting bored. A well-dressed bloke, eager for some easy fun, comes up to her and says: 'Let's have a game. I'm going to ask you a question. If you can't answer it, you'll give me £5. Then *you* ask me a question. If I can't answer, I'll give you £50. Is that a deal?'

The blonde thinks about it and agrees.

'Here's my question: what's the distance between the Earth and the Moon?'

The blonde doesn't even bother to try. She reaches in her purse for a fiver and gives it to the guy.

'OK; my question now,' she says. 'What's red and blue and jumps all over the place?'

The guy thinks about it for several long minutes but, eventually, he must admit he doesn't have a clue. Grudgingly, he gives the blonde £50, which she pockets with a smile.

'Hold on a minute!' the guy says. 'What *is* red and blue and jumps all over the place?'

The blonde looks at him and wordlessly hands him a fiver.

A TOUCH OF SOMETHING

A brunette goes to see her GP with an unusual problem.

'I can't understand what's wrong with me,' she tells him. 'Wherever I touch myself, it hurts. My nose hurts. My leg hurts, my foot hurts, my ass hurts – everything hurts.' And to emphasise her point, she pokes herself at the various places she's just mentioned.

The doctor thinks for a minute then says: 'Tell me; did you used to be a blonde?'

'Why, yes, I just dyed my hair so that people would stop making silly jokes about me.'

'I know what's wrong with you. Your finger is broken.'

BUT OF COURSE...

What do you say to a blonde with no arms and no legs?

Nice tits.

NICE TRY, BUSTER

A guy has been sitting in a bar for 20 minutes, looking at a blonde who's wearing the tightest pair of pants he's ever seen. They fit her butt to perfection, but he's wondering how on earth she manages to fit it in them. After the third beer, curiosity takes over from propriety and he walks over to her.

'Tell me,' he asks her, 'how do you get into these pants?'

The young blonde looks him over with an appreciative smile and replies: 'Well, you could start by buying me a drink.'

JUST TO MAKE SURE

How do you know a blonde sent you a fax?

There's a stamp on it.

BEYOND A JOKE

A blonde manages to persuade her brunette sister to take her out. Not knowing where to go and not wanting to let the people she usually hangs out with know she has a blonde sister, the brunette decides to drive her to a small club where they might have suitable entertainment for her sister.

They sit down and order some drinks, they talk about this and that and after a few minutes a ventriloquist sits down on a chair on the stage.

'Hello, Harry,' he says to the puppet on his knees. 'Do you have any good jokes for us?' and the puppet starts delivering the most outrageous blonde jokes ever uttered by a ventriloquist.

This is too much for the blonde, who stands up and starts shouting: 'Oh, come on! Being a blonde doesn't necessarily mean you're stupid. I find this act very insulting and I'm going to complain to the manager.'

'Ah, I'm sorry, young lady,' the ventriloquist stammers. 'Harry didn't mean to be offensive…'

'You stay out of it, buster,' the incensed blonde cuts him off. 'I'm not talking to you; I'm talking to the little guy.'

MIZZ FRIZZ

What do blondes do after they comb their hair?

They pull up their knickers.

A MAN WROTE THIS JOKE

What's the difference between a pit-bull and a blonde with PMT?

Lipstick.

TURTLEY HILARIOUS

Why is a blonde like a turtle?

They're both fucked when they're on their back.

HOT STUFF

A blonde enters a sex shop. She browses around and stops in front of the dildo section, but apparently she can't really make her mind up.

'I'm sorry; it was the holidays and we're a bit short of stock at the moment', the sales assistant tells her. 'We still have a few behind the counter, if you'd like to have a look.'

The blonde agrees and is shown a nice, pink, glittery dildo.

'How much is it?' the blonde asks.

The sales assistant replies, '£20'.

'What about this one?'

'This one's £35. It's a special one: you bung it in the microwave before you use it.'

'Oooohh... and how much for this big silver and black one at the back?'

'Er, that's my Thermos flask, madam.'

IT'S, LIKE, SO OBVIOUS

Two blondes are walking in the beautiful Australian outback. One of them asks the other: 'I wonder which is further... London or the Moon?'

The other blonde looks at her in amazement.

'Hell-*o*! Can you see London from here?'

OH, NOW I GET IT

A blonde goes to a hardware store and says to the sales assistant: 'I'd like to buy this TV, please.'

'I'm sorry. We don't sell to blondes; that's company policy.'

The blonde is incensed but the guy is adamant, so she goes back home fuming. After a while, she devises a cunning plan: she's going to dye her hair and pass as a brunette.

Thus attired, she goes back to the hardware shop.

'I'd like to buy this TV, please.'

'I'm sorry. We don't sell to blondes; that's company policy,' replies the guy again.

Angry, but most of all puzzled, the blonde decides to turn herself into a redhead and come back a bit later in the week.

A few days later, her head a flaming mass of auburn curls, she goes back to the shop and asks to buy the TV again. Again the salesman refuses to sell her anything on account of her being a blonde.

'But how on earth do you know I'm a blonde? I changed my hair twice and I'm not wearing the same clothes!'

'Because that's a microwave,' the guy replies with a sigh.

NOT AS DUMB AS SHE LOOKS

The casino is nearly empty and these two croupiers are getting pretty bored when a blonde turns up at their roulette table. She flutters her eyelashes at them and whispers breathlessly that she'd like to have a go.

'I hope this isn't against company policy, but I feel luckier when I'm naked,' she tells the two guys.

They look around at the deserted casino and tell her that it shouldn't be a problem. The blonde then takes her clothes off and bets a thousand pounds on a single roll of the ball. The roulette wheel turns: the blonde swirls around in excitement, much to the pleasure of the two croupiers.

'Come on, come on…!' she moans, jumping up and down. 'Yes, yes… YES! I won! I won!'

She hugs both dealers and gives them a peck on the cheek, gathers up her clothes and her winnings then leaves.

The two guys look at one another, grinning like little boys.

'That was something, hey?'

'Damn right! What did she roll, anyway?'

'Hey! I thought *you* were watching!'

ON THE SCENT

Upon arriving home after work, a blonde discovers with dismay that she's been burgled. She throws herself on the sofa, mourning the loss of her stuff for a while, then calls the police. A few minutes later, a policeman knocks on her door, holding a dog on a leash in the hope of catching any scent of the burglars.

The blonde stares at the pair, then collapses on the sofa again and moans: 'Just my luck! I get burgled and they send me a blind policeman!'

MEDICAL MYSTERY

A blonde is at her GP.

'Doc, I have an unusual confession to make,' she starts. 'You see, my husband and I – well, we started experimenting with anal sex and, well, we kind of like it. Do you think this is wrong?'

'Not at all,' the doctor replies benignly. 'If you enjoy that sort of thing, go for it. As long as you stay on the pill, you'll be fine.'

'The pill? Because I can get pregnant that way too?'

'Hell, yes!' exclaims the doctor. 'Where do you think lawyers come from?'

TOTAL WRITE-OFF

There's been a horrible crash. Both cars are wrecked and smouldering. Out from under the carcase of a Volvo comes a man, stunned to find he's still alive. He looks around and, to his enormous surprise, sees the form of a blonde crawling from underneath the remnants of the BMW. They look at one another for some minutes before it dawns on them: it must be fate.

'Look,' the man breathes. 'A terrible accident and we come out unscathed. This is fate; this is God's way of telling us that we were meant for one another.'

The blonde, sensing an opening there, shakily agrees.

'And look!' the man says, pulling a bottle of miraculously

intact wine from what used to be the boot of his car. 'It didn't break! This is yet more proof that we're supposed to be together. Come on; let's have a drink together.'

The man laboriously manages to open the bottle of wine with a Swiss Army knife he always keeps in his pocket and gives the bottle to the blonde, who takes a healthy swig.

'And you; you're not drinking?' she asks the guy.

'Oh, no. I'd rather wait for the police.'

ONE A DAY

A young and precocious blonde is going to see her GP.

'I'd like to go on the pill, doctor. I'm afraid I might get pregnant when I have sex,' she tells him.

'Yes; that's a very sensible thing to do,' replies the GP, somewhat surprised at the blonde's apparent maturity. She performs a few tests and gives her a prescription. 'Pop one pill every day and you'll be fine.'

A week later, the blonde comes back and looks rather flustered.

'Doctor, it's about this pill thing.'

'Yes?'

'It keeps falling out!'

WHAT YOU SEE IS WHAT YOU GET

A guy is angry with his blonde girlfriend. Time and time again he's asked her not to use his computer because she keeps on messing up his work.

'Please don't touch the computer. I use it for work and it's very important,' he tells her.

The blonde contritely agrees and a week passes. One day the guy comes back from work, sits down at his keyboard to check his email and have a quick game before dinner.

'Honey, you've been messing with my computer again,' he tells his girlfriend after a while.

Unable to lie, she says that yes, she has. 'But how do you know?'

'There's Tippex all over the screen and the joystick's wet,' he sighs in despair.

A BIT OF A BOOB

A blonde is coming back from school one day. She saunters into the kitchen where her mum is preparing dinner and says: 'Mum, Mum; I can count up to ten!' and she demonstrates: 'One, two, three…'

When she is done, her mum is full of pride for her. 'Well done, honey! It's because you're a blonde that you can do stuff like that.'

Full of love for her mum, the blonde has a great evening and goes to bed happy. The following day she comes back from school and says: 'Mum, Mum, I learned the alphabet today! Listen: a, b, c, d….'

'What a big girl you are, sweetie-pie. I'm so very proud of you.'

'Is it because I'm a blonde that I can do all this stuff?'

'Yes, of course it is, dear.'

At peace with the universe, the blonde goes to bed with a light heart. The following day, she comes back from school chanting: 'Mum, Mum, look at these!', pulling up her sweater and revealing a magnificent pair of boobs.

'None of the girls at school has boobs that big! Is that because I'm a blonde too?'

'No, dear, replies her mum with an apologetic smile. 'That's because you're 24.'

A NIP IN THE AIR

A policeman is walking down the street when he spots a blonde. Upon closer inspection, he realises that this blonde has the front of her blouse open and one of her breasts is hanging out.

He goes up to her and says: 'Lady, I could book you for indecent exposure! Please cover yourself!'

The blonde looks at him uncomprehendingly and then looks down.

'Oh my God!' she exclaims. 'I left the baby on the bus!'

ANSWERS ON A POSTCARD

What do you call a blonde blowing in another blonde's ear?

Data transfer.

FULL OF SURPRISES

What did the blonde call her pet zebra?

Spot.

WHERE ARE THEY NOW?

Fifteen years after they left school, a group of students meet again to discuss what has happened to them so far in their lives. They all gather in a pub for a drink.

'So, how are you doing?' Bob asks another student.

'Me? I'm doing quite well, thank you. I'm the CEO of a company that sells computers and we're one of the biggest companies in Britain!'

'Well done mate! Me, I'm a university professor now and I've written a couple of books that are selling quite well,' says Bob.

They all congratulate themselves on the great life they have. One is a famous lawyer, another is becoming a renowned actress… then Bob notices Harry's here, the black sheep of the lot, the one who was always at the back of the class near the radiator. He also notices that all the guys who go and see him for a chat seem to leave with rather strained smiles on their lips, while Harry looks pretty smug. He's got a great-looking blonde girl on his knees, who obviously dotes on him. Overcome with curiosity, Bob leans towards his friend and asks: 'What about Harry?'

'Well, Harry's doing OK,' his friend replies in an envious voice. 'See that blonde? He's married to her. She's deaf and mute and we're sitting in her dad's pub.'

WATCHING MY WEIGHT

A blonde is sitting in a restaurant. She's ordered a pizza and when it arrives, she realises it's absolutely huge.

'Shall I cut it into six or 12?' asks the waiter.

'Oh, into six, please,' she replies. 'I couldn't possibly eat 12 pieces!'

CLUE: IT'S ABOUT SEX

Why do blondes prefer driving convertibles?

More legroom.

GETTING THE PICTURE

'Hey, look!' the blonde says to her boyfriend. 'You should be proud of me! I managed to finish this Disney jigsaw puzzle in far less time than the average person!'

'But it took you five months!' her boyfriend laughs.

'Yeah, but on the box it says "Three to five years"!'

GOING ROUND IN CIRCLES

A policeman has been following this car for a while and the driver's been swerving across the road for the last ten minutes in a most dangerous manner. The policeman puts his flashing lights on and forces the car to stop.

'Did you realise that you've been swerving across the road for the last ten minutes? You nearly crashed into oncoming traffic twice and scratched at least two parked cars! What's the matter with you?'

'I'm sorry, officer,' replies the blonde driver. 'I saw this tree in the middle of the street, so I turned to avoid it: then there was another one, so I turned again, and there was another one – I mean, whose idea was it to plant trees right in the middle of the road, eh?'

'Madam,' says the policeman in a tired tone, 'That's your air freshener.'

CIRCLES OF YOUR MIND

What did the blonde say when she looked into a box of Cheerios?

'Oh, look! Doughnut seeds!'

HARSH BUT FAIR

A group of girls are sitting at the terrace of a bar laughing uproariously and chanting '24, 24, 24!'

A blonde walks by and stops, a smile on her face: it looks like a birthday party of some sort.

'You guys seem to be having fun,' she tells them. 'You're celebrating something?'

'Yeah, you could say that,' one of them answers. 'Wanna join in?'

'Sure.' The blonde finds an empty seat, gets a drink and starts chanting '24, 24, 24!' with the rest of the girls.

'You know,' one of them says, 'it's even funnier if you do it in the middle of the street.'

The blonde gets up, proud to have been included in such a band of merry people, and goes to stand in the middle of the road... where she is quickly run over by a lorry.

The girls at the terrace all howl with laughter and start chanting: '25, 25, 25!'

CHAUVINIST PIG

A blonde is walking in a funfair with a pig on a leash. A guy, attracted by the prospect of an easy pull, goes up to her and asks: 'Where did you get that?'

'I won her in a raffle,' replies the pig.

EASY MISTAKE TO MAKE

Due to a tear in the very fabric of the matrix of the universe, a blonde finds herself attending a science conference about global warming. She gets quite bored and doesn't understand a word of what is being said, but the conference soon finishes and she's eyeing up a good-looking bloke at the bar.

'Hiya!' she says, flashing a ravishing smile. 'Do you come here often?'

'Er, not really,' replies the scientist. 'This isn't really my speciality.'

'Ooh,' exclaims the blonde with a little wicked twinkle in her eyes. 'And what *is* your speciality exactly?'

'I specialise in nuclear fission.'

'Cool! And what do you use for bait?'

OH, SHIT

A blonde has had a baby. She is very proud of the tiny thing and swears she's going to take care of her and love her.

She goes back home after the delivery and her husband instals her on the sofa while he goes to check that everything is ready for the new baby. 'I'm so proud of you, honey! What a wonderful baby you've given us.'

The blonde is over the moon and spends the next few days in contentment, until her husband notices a bad smell in the cot. He leans forward and feels about and realises in horror that the baby is covered in shit.

'Honey, what's happened? Didn't you change the baby's nappy?'

'It's all right, darling; I checked! It says on the box. 'Suitable for up to twenty pounds.'

MYSTERY SOLVED

Why don't blondes eat jelly?

Because they can't figure out how to fit the pint of water into that little package.

WE'VE ALL BEEN THERE

How can you tell that a blonde's having a bad day?

She has a tampon tucked behind her ear and she can't find her pencil.

WORTH ITS WEIGHT IN GOLD

A man goes to Russia one day and, in a back alley near Red Square, he stumbles across a black-market brain stall.

Spotting the foreign tourist, the seedy-looking trader says: 'Doctor's brain, $10 an ounce.'

'I don't need a doctor's brain,' the guy laughs.

'Lawyer's brain. Nice and fresh: $20 an ounce.'

'What do you want me to do with a lawyer's brain?' the guy replies.

'You are hard man to please,' the trader says. 'Here: blonde brain, $100 an ounce.'

'A hundred dollars? How come it's much more expensive than a doctor's brain or even a lawyer's brain?'

The trader looks at him and shakes his head. 'You have any idea how many blondes I have to kill to get ounce of brain?'

EMPTY-HEADED

How do you make a blonde's eyes sparkle?

Shine a flashlight in her ear.

DADDY'S GIRL

The blonde bride, upon her engagement, went to her mother and said: 'I've found a man just like father!'

'So what do you want from me: sympathy?' her mother replied.

BASKET CASE

What's the difference between a blonde and a supermarket trolley?

Supermarket trolleys have a mind of their own.

PNEUMATIC

What do you call a blonde lying flat on her back?

An air mattress.

EASY MISTAKE

A blonde is trying to get back home, but she's caught in a really nasty blizzard. She remembers somebody having told her once that when such a thing happens the best thing to do is to wait for the snow plough to turn up, then follow it. So she waits for an hour and, finally, a snow plough arrives. Dutifully, she starts the engine and follows it. She follows it for half an hour, going round in circles behind it, when the driver of the snow plough comes down from his cabin and approaches her car.

'OK, I've finished with the Safeway car park, lady,' he tells her. 'Do you want to follow me next door to Homebase?'

CAN DO

A blonde is looking at the male deodorant section in a shop. Dazzled by the sheer number of products she can buy and unable to remember what her husband usually wears, she goes to find a sales assistant.

'I need to buy some deodorant for my husband,' she tells him.

'Ball or aerosol?'

'Nah; it's for under his arms.'

WOMEN: KNOW YOUR LIMITS

Why did the blonde crash into the ditch?

She left her indicator on.

FORCE OF HABIT

Why can't blondes pass their driving tests?

Because every time the car stops they jump in the back seat.

A HAIRY SITUATION

A blonde has been invited over to a friend's for a drink. She can't help noticing that her friend's husband, who usually has dandruff all over him, has now clean and shiny hair.

'I don't want to sound rude,' she says to her friend, 'but Harry's hair looks far better now.'

'Yes, I know. We tried loads of shampoos and stuff, and then one day I gave him Head and Shoulders and it all went away.'

'Oh? And how do you give shoulders?' the blonde asks innocently.

HIGHER THOUGHTS

What's the difference between a prostitute, a nymphomaniac, and a blonde?

The prostitute says: 'Aren't you done yet?'

The nympho says: 'Are you done already?'

The blonde says: 'White... I think I'll paint the ceiling white after all.'

IN YOUR DREAMS

A dumb blonde, a smart blonde and Santa Claus are walking down the street at Christmas one day and stumble upon a fiver lying on the pavement. Question: Who picks it up?

Answer: The dumb blonde. The other two don't exist.

THIRD OPTION

A brunette, a redhead and a blonde are attending an antenatal class. They'd all like to know what their baby is going to be: a boy or a girl. The doctor in charge tells them that it all depends on the sexual position adopted when the baby was conceived.

'He was on top,' the brunette says.

'Then the chances are that you're going to deliver a boy, my dear young woman.'

'When we decided to make a baby, *I* was on top,' declares the redhead.

'Well, the chances are that you'll have a baby girl,' the doctor explains.

They all turn to the blonde, who looks disconsolate.

'Does that mean I'm gonna have puppies?'

OOH... THAT SMARTS!

What do you get if you dye a blonde into a brunette?

Artificial intelligence.

ONE MUST HAVE STANDARDS

A blonde is sitting in her living room painting her nails when the phone rings. There is a hush at the other end of the line and a wheezing voice asks: 'Hey, lady; try to guess what I'm holding in my hand!'

'My dear man, if it fits in one hand, I'm not interested,' she replies and hangs up.

GRIEVED AND BEREAVED

Eleanor goes to visit her blonde friend Sarah, who's just lost her husband.

'I'm so sorry for you, Sarah. Is it true that you saw your husband go swimming in the pool and he drowned?'

'Yes; it was terrible.'

'Did he leave you anything in his will?'

'Five million pounds.'

'Five million pounds? Not bad for someone who couldn't write…'

'… and who couldn't swim either.'

BRIGHT EYES, BURNING LIKE FIRE…

This blonde has lost both her two pet rabbits because of a strange illness. She is devastated, and decides to go and see a taxidermist. She's going to have them stuffed, so that she can remember them always.

'No problem,' says the taxidermist when the blonde explains the situation. 'Do you want them mounted?'

The blonde thinks for a couple of seconds then says: 'No, no need. Just put them face to face with their little noses touching.'

HAPPIEST DAYS OF YOUR LIFE

A blonde has mysteriously managed to get enrolled in a posh public school. The headmistress, a strict-looking affair wearing glasses and a tight bun, tells them about the rules of the school, and particularly the need for sexual abstinence.

'You'll have to control these appetites,' she says to the girls gathered in the hall. 'After all, do you really want an hour of pleasure to spoil a whole school career?'

The blonde raises her hand and asks innocently: 'Miss, how do you make it last an hour?'

GAME, SET AND SNATCH

This blonde wants to get married to a millionaire. The guy is a catch, but he's got some strange notions about sex: he wants his bride to be a virgin. Unfortunately, our blonde hasn't been a virgin since she was 16, so she goes to see her doctor.

'I see your problem,' the doctor says. 'Believe it or not, this isn't such an unusual request from a groom-to-be. There are two ways to go about it: one will cost you £1,000 and you'll need to be with us for at least a week, while the other will only cost you £50 and I can perform the operation right now. Both operations will have the same result in terms of pain and blood and the rest.'

The blonde thinks about it and decides that if she could afford the £1,000 operation, she wouldn't need to marry a millionaire, so she goes for the cheaper option. The doctor makes her lie down on the examination table and busies himself around her crotch area for 20 minutes, then pockets the £50.

A couple of weeks later, the blonde comes back to see her doctor a happily married woman.

'It was great, doctor: thank you! It was perfect, in fact. On our wedding night, it was like losing my virginity again. What did you do to me?'

'Oh, it's really quite simple,' the doctor said with a smile. 'I braided your pubic hair together.'

WRITE ON AT LEAST ONE SIDE OF THE PAPER

A blonde has to fill in a form. The prospect is daunting, but she breathes deeply and sits down at the table with a flask of coffee, a pencil and three erasers.

'First Name'. Now, that one's quite easy. She checks on her passport and writes down her name.

'Surname'. An easy one again. She dutifully writes down her name.

'Sex'. She thinks for a while and has some coffee, then writes down 'Three times a week.'

LYING DOWN ON THE JOB

Why would a blonde walk around with a mattress?

She's carrying her CV.

Chapter 4
Political jokes

Some of these are not, strictly speaking, jokes. These are real statements by George W. Bush. That's what makes them funny … yes, and scary too …

'I hope you leave here and walk out and say, "What did he say?"' *August 13, 2004*

'Let me put it to you bluntly. In a changing world, we want more people to have control over your own life.' *August 9, 2004*

'I'm honoured to shake the hand of a brave Iraqi citizen who had his hand cut off by Saddam Hussein.' *May 25, 2004*

'We're still being challenged in Iraq and the reason why is a free Iraq will be a major defeat in the cause of freedom.' *April 5, 2004*

'The most important job is not to be governor, or first lady in my case.' *January 30, 2004*

'I know the human being and fish can coexist peacefully.' *September 29, 2000*

'They misunderestimated me.' *November 6, 2000*

'When I take action, I'm not going to fire a $2 million missile at a $10 empty tent and hit a camel in the butt. It's going to be decisive.' *September 19, 2001*

'It's my honour to speak to you as the leader of your country. And the great thing about America is you don't have to listen unless you want to.' *July 10, 2001*

'I'm hopeful. I know there is a lot of ambition in Washington, obviously. But I hope the ambitious realise that they are more likely to succeed with success as opposed to failure.' *January 18, 2001*

'There's only one person who hugs the mothers and the widows, the wives and the kids upon the death of their loved one. Others hug but having committed the troops, I've got an additional responsibility to hug and that's me and I know what it's like.' *December 11, 2002*

'There's an old saying in Tennessee – I know it's in Texas, probably in Tennessee – that says, "Fool me once, shame on – shame on you. Fool me – you can't get fooled again."' *September 17, 2002*

'I just want you to know that, when we talk about war, we're really talking about peace.' *June 18, 2002*

'We've tripled the amount of money – I believe it's from $50 million up to $195 million available.' *March 23, 2002*

'The ambassador and the general were briefing me on the – the vast majority of Iraqis want to live in a peaceful, free world. And we will find these people and we will bring them to justice.' October 27, 2003

'I'm the master of low expectations.' June 4, 2003

KGP

President Bush is in Russia for a state visit to his Soviet counterpart. He goes and visits the Red Square and gets lost. He spends hours rambling in the streets of Moscow and, after a while, he feels the urge to urinate. He holds it for as long as he can, but eventually has to relent and unbuttons his fly against a wall.

'What you doing here?' a Russian policeman asks him, obviously not pleased at this tourist – and an American tourist at that, judging by his clothes – peeing in Mother Russia's finest city.

'Come on, man, I really need to!' squirms Bush, dancing on the spot.

'You can't do here. Follow me.'

The policeman leads the way to a beautiful park, full of flowers and fountains. He points at a wall: 'You do here.'

Relieved, Bush lets go with delight. When he's done, he turns around and asks the Russian policeman: 'Thank you for taking me here. Is this Russian hospitality?'

'No,' the guy replies with a broad smile. 'This be American Embassy.'

BAD CONSTITUTION

Bush recently went for a heart examination.

It came back negative.

IN GOB WE TRUST

Bush is considering his own image in the mirror and reflects that he's not such a bad-looking guy after all. He's pretty cool. In fact, he's so cool that there should be a way to show Americans how cool he is. He thinks about it for an hour or so and comes up with an idea: he's going to have a stamp printed with his portrait on it!

Being the boss, he passes a new Bill (the GW Stamp Bill) and soon billions of stamps with his face on them are flooding the USA. After a week, though, his administration receives tons of complaints from the post office: the stamp doesn't stick. An enquiry is started, which comes back with this astonishing result: people kept on spitting on the wrong side of the stamp.

PUT YOUR LITTER HERE

A secret agent is walking down Central Park when he spots a little boy carrying a box. Times being what they are in America, he decides to have a closer look.

'Good morning, little boy; what have you got in your box?'

'Kittens, sir,' says the little boy with enthusiasm. 'Brand-new American kittens. They were born a few hours ago.'

'That's cute,' the guy says. He congratulates the little boy and leaves.

Later on in the day, the secret agent is back at the White House. He spots the little boy again, sitting on the steps near the entrance, taking the sun and peering into the box from time to time. With a grin, he decides to tell the President.

'Mister President, Sir, there's something you might want to see. It's a little boy who's got American kittens.'

President Bush dabs at his face, full of crumbs from lunch, and follows the guy outside. They walk up to the little boy, who stands up when he sees who's coming.

'What have you got in this box?' asks GW Bush.

'New kittens, Sir,' the little boy replies. 'Brand-new Canadian kittens.'

'Canadians?' the secret agent frowns, 'I thought you said they were American kittens?'

'Well, yeah; but their eyes are open now.'

GEORGE W WHOOSH!

A guy is driving back home after a hard day at the Pentagon when he's caught in a jam. The traffic is at a total standstill. He remains trapped in there for an hour before a busy-looking policeman comes up to his car.

'What's up, officer?'

'Well, it's the President, sir,' replies the officer. 'He's feeling a bit low: he says that nobody understands that we needed to go to war in Iraq and that he's not just doing what his wealthy friends are telling him to do and that he's a real President... You know what I mean... So he's sitting in the middle of the street up there threatening to douse himself in petrol and immolate himself if the American people don't show him they love him. We're doing a collection for him now, sir.'

'Really? And how much have you got so far?'

'Well, a lot of people are siphoning, so we've managed to get nearly a hundred gallons so far.'

THAT'S MORE LIKE IT

An MP is trying his best to vote down a legal proposal by Blair's government. He feels very frustrated and explodes: 'Half of this House is made up of cowards and the other half is corrupt!'

He is instantly booed by his colleagues and threatened with being barred and losing his office if he doesn't apologise right away.

'OK,' he says. 'Half of this House is *not* made of cowards and the other half is *not* corrupt.'

BE CAREFUL WHAT YOU WISH FOR

A Canadian, President Bush and Osama bin Laden are talking together in an attempt to bring peace to the world.

They walk far into the desert, so that no one will interrupt them, when they stumble across an old-looking lamp. The Canadian picks it up and has a go at cleaning it. A genie pops out of the lamp and says he will grant each of them one wish to thank them for delivering him from 1,000 years of imprisonment.

As the Canadian is here for comic relief, really, he decides to make a point of it and show that peace can be achieved with goodwill in the world.

'I would like Canada to be a happy and fertile land,' he requests from the genie.

The genie nods his approval and concentrates. There is a flash of light and the whole of Canada becomes a rich, luscious land full of happy people.

President Bush is not impressed by this and thinks the Canadian guy is a bit soppy.

'I wish for a wall: an impenetrable wall all around America, so that no one can come in and hurt us.'

The genie nods and, in a flash of light, creates a huge monster of a wall, 50 metres high, all around America.

Osama bin Laden muses for a minute and asks the genie: 'This wall around America: it is really tight?'

The genie nods.

'I mean, no one or nothing can get in or out?'

The genie nods again.

'Fill it with water,' he orders the genie.

GEORGE W HUSH

Bush enters a library.

'I'd like a burger and fries, please,' he says.

'Shhh. Quieter: this is a library!'

'Oh: sorry. Could I have a burger and fries, please?' the President whispers.

A BOOT DU SOUFFLE

Tony Blair and Jacques Chirac are having a meal one day and they argue over who should pay the bill. Both are adamant that it is their turn to pay and the fight goes on for 20 minutes before Jacques Chirac holds up his hand.

'Bien… we can't agree, so we'll have to settle it the French way.'

'What do you mean, the French way?' Tony asks, not trusting the Frenchman.

'Well, in France, when two men can't resolve their difference, they take it in turns to kick one another in the balls until there's only one man standing. The man who's still up has proved he's a real man and therefore the other one must submit to his rules.'

Well, it's quite difficult for Tony Blair to wriggle out of this one, as it will look like he's not a real man if he does, so he agrees.

'I'm the eldest here, so I will kick you first: then it will be your turn.'

Blair isn't too happy about this but, once again, he agrees, in deference to Chirac's age. He braces himself and closes his eyes… and Jacques Chirac delivers a mighty kick to the groin that drives the Prime Minister to his knees. His bollocks are on fire, he can't breathe, the world is spinning, but after a few minutes he can stand up.

'Right,' he croaks. 'Now it's my turn.'

'Nah,' the French President replies with a grin. 'I lose. You can pay.'

JUDGEMENT DAY

George W Bush dies. It took too long to happen, but at last he's gone, and approaching the Pearly Gates.

Saint Peter is there, guarding the door and deciding where to direct the poor souls, whether to Heaven or Hell. He sees the Prez walking up to him and strokes his bearded chin.

'President Bush,' he says. 'You've done pretty weird things in your life and it is quite difficult for our administration here to know what to do with you. We can't decide whether you're a complete moron or whether you knew what you were doing back down on Earth. That's why we've decided to give you a choice.' He looks at Dubya intently. 'You are going to be allowed a tour, which is not something we do very often here. You'll spend one day in Hell and one day in Heaven. At the end of this tour, you'll have to choose where you want to spend the rest of eternity.'

President Bush nods and Saint Peter takes him to a hole in the cloud from which a flight of stairs is going down. Bush looks back at Saint Peter, who encourages him with a gentle push. Down he goes.

After what feels an eternity, he arrives at a pair of wide iron doors. There is a neon sign above them that read 'Hell' in garish red letters. His heart pounding, he gets ready to knock when the doors suddenly open inwards.

'Welcome to Hell!' a committee of scantily-clad ladies cries out when they see him. Dubya can't believe his eyes. In front of him stretches an enormous cave, all lit up with neon signs written 'Sex' and 'Bar' and 'Republican Convention' in blinking letters, like a Christmas shopping mall gone crazy. There are Jamaican beats and congo drums and all he can hear is laughter and people having a great time. The men are all dressed in Hawaiian shirts and nurse pina coladas while the women wear low-cut dresses showing off their attributes. The Devil himself is here to greet him, a big grin on his face, his horns adorned with two flashing stars. He approaches Bush and shoves a drink into his hand.

'Uh… I don't drink anymore,' says the Prez. 'I gave it up a while ago.'

'Relax!' says the Devil. 'Here, everything's allowed. You can drink, screw, eat whatever you want, wherever you want, whenever you want! It won't count with upstairs either. For one day, you're absolutely free, so make the best of it!'

Bush thinks about it and says to himself: 'Heck, why not? I can have a good time too. Being President of the World hasn't been fun every day.'

He takes the drink and has a sip. The Devil takes him by the shoulder in a very friendly manner. 'I'll give you a tour, man. You've earned some rest and some fun. We're going to have a whale of a time.'

For a whole day and a night Bush is treated like a king. He eats caviar and lobster and drinks champagne. He goes to a show where Jacques Chirac is being buggered by Kofi Annan and he's never laughed so hard in his life. He meets famous people: Nixon is nearly comatose with drink, Dillinger has a bevy of immoral young women attending to his needs and he even has a go in a tank, shooting mangy-looking naked Iraqis running around like rabbits. All he's ever wanted to do in his life he can do now with all impunity. People come to him and greet him with smiles and drinks, he makes loads of friends, women make broad passes at him and, in the morning, the Devil wakes him up from the arms of a teenage ex-virgin to show him out. There's a crowd gathered at the iron gates and they all wave him off good-naturedly. 'See you later, friend!' shouts the Devil before closing the doors.

'Well, that wasn't so bad,' Dubya thinks. He feels invigorated – he doesn't even have a hangover – and walks up the steps to the Pearly Gates to meet Saint Peter again.

Without a word, Saint Peter shows him to another hole in the clouds with a flight of steps, this time going up to Heaven.

Bush soon arrives at a small iron gate beyond which extends a magnificent garden, lush with life and colours. He is greeted by Jesus himself who talks to him in a calm and engaging voice: 'Welcome to Heaven, my dear friend. You will spend an entire day here with us and see the wonders peace and love can do to your soul.'

So for a whole day and a night President Bush meets famous people of the likes of Mother Theresa, Princess Diana and President Kennedy. He talks about a lot of very profound and intellectual things, few of which he understands. Everybody is nice and polite and witty and evidently cares for the world and the souls of their neighbours. Bush eats delicious salads and drinks the purest water he has ever tasted in his years as a teetotaller, a welcome break from his binge the previous night. In the morning, he is woken up by the wet touch of the nose of an adoring lamb on his cheek. Jesus picks him up and says: 'It was nice of you to come, President Bush. We all appreciate your visit: you are a rare man. I must return you to our revered gatekeeper now.'

Dazzled by the purity and the beauty of what he has seen, Bush returns to meet Saint Peter for the third time.

'So, what will it be, my son?' asks Saint Peter. 'Heaven or Hell?'

'Well,' Dubya answers after collecting his thoughts, 'You know, I'd never thought I'd say that but... You know, Jesus and Heaven: it's great but... a bit boring, now? I mean, don't get me wrong: the people up there are lovely and all, but there's no real entertainment if you see what I mean. And Jesus is... well, I thought he was white, but he looks like a Jewish hippy to me with all his peace and love talk, you know... If I have to spend all eternity somewhere, I'd rather have some fun, if you get my meaning. So yeah, I guess I'm gonna go for Hell.'

'So be it,' intones Saint Peter and shows him to the little hole in the clouds with a staircase that goes down.

Bush rushes down the stairs two at a time, eager to get to party, and soon arrives at the huge iron gates again. 'Bring it on,' he thinks to himself and watches with delight the great doors opening for him.

He is not prepared to see what he sees now. The huge cave is now dark and dirty, populated by demons doing very unsavoury things to people: prodding them, biting them, kicking them. A guy he recognises from the previous party is being whipped repeatedly while he's carrying the carcase of a large beast dripping blood. There is no music, only the cries of pain and the low moans of suffering.

'I don't understand,' he says to the Devil, who's come to greet him with a nasty-looking hooked pitchfork. 'Yesterday we were eating caviar and drinking champagne, we were having fun and all and now… this?'

'Ah, but you see, yesterday we were campaigning,' the Devil purrs in his ears. 'Today, you voted for us.'

DIVIDED BY A COMMON LANGUAGE

Americans have a funny way with words. They say 'elevator'; we say 'lift'. They say 'fries'; we say 'chips'. They say 'President'; we say 'homicidal psycho maniacal git'.

IF YOU WANT A JOB DONE PROPERLY…

President Bush is in trouble. The famed weapons of mass destruction have repeatedly failed to turn up. Worse, there are people who are saying now that they might not have existed at all in the first place.

Every day, Bush phones up the command centre in Iraq and asks the same question: 'Are they here yet?' Invariably, the answer is 'No.' After a couple of months, he gets desperate.

'Are they here yet?' he asks one morning.

'No, Sir; no trace of them yet.'

'How is that possible?' he explodes.

'I do have some news though, Mr President. There has

been a development to this situation since yesterday, Sir.'

'Yes?'

'Well, it appears that there's been a cock-up somewhere and that they're still in Texas, Sir. Nobody's flown them over yet.'

ETHICS FOR BEGINNERS

George Washington couldn't tell a lie.

Richard Nixon couldn't tell the truth.

George W Bush can't tell the difference.

SPELLING IT OUT

President Bush was walking around Buckingham Palace in the company of the Queen one day. She could sense there was something on his mind and, after a while, he blurted out: 'You know what? You're the head of a kingdom. That's very cool. It gives you standing. I'd like to be the head of a kingdom.'

'Yes, but you can't, my dear,' replied the Queen. 'To be the head of a kingdom, you need a king. That's where the word comes from: king-dom. You aren't a king, so you can't lead a kingdom.'

'What about an empire?'

'It's the same thing, as I'm sure you understand. An empire requires an emperor.'

'And a principality? I could make do with a principality,' said Dubya hopefully.

'You can't, I'm afraid,' tutted the Queen. 'You'd need to be a prince to run a principality.'

'What about…?'

'My dear,' the Queen interrupted, 'believe me. Forget about your dreams of aristocracy. You are the right man to run a country.'

OUT OF THE MOUTHS OF BABES...

President Bush is touring the country campaigning for re-election. He ends up in a school where the teacher asks him shyly if he would like to spend some time doing a vocabulary exercise with the children.

'Maybe you could help me explain what a tragedy is.'

'Sure thing; bring it on,' says the Prez.

'Children, we are going to try to see if we can define what a tragedy is. The President here is going to help us in our discussion.'

The class is silent for a moment: then a bright-looking little girl puts her hand up.

'If I was walking the dog and a car ran over him, would it be a tragedy?'

'Ah, no,' said the President. 'It would be called an accident.'

'What if a bus was to drive over a cliff and kill all the kids inside? Would that be a tragedy?' asks another pupil.

'We're getting there,' congratulated Bush. 'It wouldn't be quite a tragedy. It would be a great loss.'

The class is silent once more: then a little boy raises his hand.

'If you were flying in Air Force One and you were gunned down by a missile and you got dead, would that be a tragedy?'

'Yes, absolutely; you're right!' exclaims the President. 'And tell me, why do you think it would be a tragedy?'

'Well,' says the little boy, thinking hard. 'It wouldn't be a great loss, but it probably wouldn't be an accident either.'

A LONG WAY DOWN

The Pope, Tony Blair and George W Bush are on a plane, trying to discuss world peace, when one of the engines fails. Soon the second engine fails as well and they're plummeting to their deaths. There are only three parachutes in the plane, but four people on board, including the pilot.

Quick as a hawk, Bush grabs a parachute and declares: 'I'm the President of the United States, the most powerful man on the planet. I have to survive to carry on fighting for freedom.' He opens the plane's door and jumps. Tony Blair, just as quick, grabs another parachute and says: 'This man who just jumped showed judgement. I have to follow in the steps of such a man, for the perpetuity of British values.' He, too, jumps.

There is only one parachute left, and the pilot hands it over to the pontiff. 'Here, Your Holiness: you jump.'

'Worry not, my son,' the Pope chuckles. 'George grabbed the lunchbox.'

NATURE'S WAY

Bush Senior and Bush Junior are out hunting. After a whole day out, they finally slaughter a deer. The beast is magnificent, with large, imposing antlers which will go nicely next to Saddam Hussein's beard on the Oval Office wall.

The two men are going back to the truck when another

hunter walks by. They exchange greetings and, after a while, the old hunter tells them: 'Fellas, you know, it'd be far better if you dragged the deer the other way, so that the antlers don't dig into the ground.'

The Bushes look around at the deer and realise that the old guy has a point. They thank him and carry on with their task.

'You know,' Senior says to Junior, 'this guy was right. It's much easier to drag a deer this way.'

'Yeah,' Dubya pants, 'but we're getting even further away from the truck now.'

A NARROW ESCAPE

Saddam Hussein is sipping tea in his palace one day when he receives a phone call.

'This is Shaun, from Ireland,' the voice says. 'Me and my mates at the White Horse pub have decided that you are a thoroughly evil person and we're declaring war on you.'

Saddam Hussein is quite taken aback but, after the first shock, decides to play along.

'As you wish, Mister Shaun. But I have to tell you that I have an army of a million men ready to fight for me.'

'Mmmm…' Shaun says. 'I see. OK, I'll come back to you on that one.' Sure enough, an hour or so later Saddam Hussein receives another phone call from Shaun.

'Right,' says Shaun. 'We've managed to get hold of some equipment, so we're much stronger now. We now officially declare war on you.'

'What kind of equipment are you talking about, Sir?'

'We got Dermot's tractor and the guvnor's bulldozer.

That'll do nicely as infantry vehicles, wouldn't you think?' The voice at the end of the line sounds smug, if somewhat slurry.

'I think you do not understand, Sir,' replies Saddam Hussein, quite enjoying himself. 'I have warplanes, all equipped with the latest American technology, mobile missile batteries, Russian tanks, bazookas…'

'Mmmm… I see,' Shaun says. 'I'll come back to you.'

An hour passes and the phone rings again.

'Right,' says Shaun. 'We've enlisted the crew at the King's Head now, so we've doubled our numbers. We also have a modified glider with a pair of shotguns on each wing and some dynamite we kept for Bonfire Night. What do you say about that hey?'

'Well, I admire your resourcefulness, Mister Shaun, but I have increased the size of my army to two million people since we last spoke,' says Saddam Hussein, laughing to tears. 'I also bought a couple of carriers and I have ordered the production of weapons of mass destruction, just in case my two million-strong army is not up to the job.'

'Two million, you say?' mulls Shaun. 'OK, I'll get back to you.'

Another hour passes. Saddam Hussein is starting to think he's not going to hear from Shaun any more when the phone rings. Delighted, he picks up the receiver.

'Right,' says Shaun. 'Me and my mates have decided to postpone declaring war on you,' he announces.

'Oh, really?' Saddam Hussein asks in mock wonderment. 'And why would that be?'

'Well, we've been thinking it through over a few pints and we realised there was no way we could accommodate two million prisoners.'

DARK DESIGNS

George Bush, Osama bin Laden and a good-looking young woman are seated in a train. All of a sudden the train passes through a tunnel and a ringing sound can be heard in the darkness. When they come out, Bush's left cheek is red.

Bush is thinking: 'Damn: I guess Osama had his hand up this girl's legs and she thought it was me.'

The young woman is thinking: 'I guess Bush patted Osama on the knee and got a slap for it.'

Osama bin Laden is thinking: 'Allah, be merciful. I hope there is another tunnel so I can slap Bush again.'

COLLATERAL DAMAGE

Bush and Donald Rumsfeld are sitting in a bar having a drink.

'Barman,' Bush says, 'I think I need to listen to the people here. Rumsfeld and I have a plan, but I'd like to know what you think about it, as a fellow-American.'

The barman is honoured and leans over the bar to listen to what his President has to say.

'Well, the plan's quite simple, really,' Bush starts. 'We want to invade Iraq on one spurious pretext or another, then kill at least 200,000 people and a bicycle repairman.'

'A bicycle repairman? Why on earth a bicycle repairman?'

George W Bush then turns to Rumsfeld and says: 'What did I tell you? Nobody'll care about the 200,000 Iraqis.'

TOUGH CROWD

Bush is touring again and is invited to another school one day. He's had misgivings about this sort of thing, but his advisers have told him they're good for his image, so he goes.

The classroom he enters is full of bright and eager pupils and he relaxes and is having a good time answering innocent questions when little Billy raises his hand.

'Mister President, why is it that the American Constitution is now a joke because of your Patriot Act thing? Why is it that we went to war with a country that had nothing to do with this terrorist attack on the Twin Towers? How is it that people are paying so much tax?'

The President is dumbfounded. He's totally unprepared for this and spends a minute gaping like a fish wondering what the hell he's supposed to say when, providentially, the recess bell rings.

After break, the president returns to the classroom more confident and the incident seems to be forgotten when a little girl raises her hand.

'Mister President, why is it that the American Constitution is now a joke because of your Patriot Act thing? Why is it that we went to war with a country that had nothing to do with this terrorist attack on the Twin Towers? How is it that people now are paying so much tax? And where the hell's Billy?'

VAYA CON DIOS

There has been a tragedy in Mexico. An earthquake has flattened an entire province. The world is in shock at such devastation and charity appeals are made through the

United Nations. France sends food, Canada sends equipment, Italy sends money and even the Russian and Chinese send humanitarian goods. President Bush, not to be outdone, sends 15,000 replacement Mexicans.

THROUGH THE EYES OF A CHILD

It is Valentine's Day and this little American girl, April, asks her dad: 'Dad, am I too young to send a valentine card to someone?'

Seeing that his daughter is only six, the father might answer that, yes, she might be a little too young, but he just smiles and says: 'Sweetie, no; you're not too young. If you want to send a valentine card to someone, that's fine.' He then asks, stifling a laugh: 'And tell me: who are you going to send this card to?'

'I would like to send it to Osama Bin Laden.'

The father is taken aback and chokes on the pretzel he was munching. 'April! Why on Earth would you want to send this man a valentine?'

'Well, you see, I think that if someone was to send a card to him, especially if it's coming from a little girl, he might change his ways,' she explains seriously. 'Maybe it would make him like people more and make him stop doing all the horrible things he's doing now. Maybe he hasn't had a nice mum and dad who loved him when he was a little boy. So, if he were to receive a valentine from me, maybe he would get out of where he's hiding and repent for all the bad he's done, like God tells us to do.'

The father's heart is full of pride for his little April and he gives her a big hug.

'Yes, maybe that would be an excellent idea.'

'And while he's out in the open, the Marines can beat the hell out of him,' April finishes.

DON'T DECIDE JUST YET

This is a test given recently to philosophy students in America:

This paper will place you in a fictional situation where you will have to use your judgement and react to what is happening according to the philosophical values we have learnt throughout the term.

You are a renowned news photographer. Sitting in a helicopter above Washington DC, you are witnessing a humanitarian disaster: an earthquake has wiped out the entire city, which now lies in rubble in front of your camera lens. You try and capture the agony, the suffering and the fleetingness of existence through your art. Millions have died and millions are still dying.

There, in the smoke and the grime, you see a form moving. You zoom in and realise it's a man. It's your President, George W Bush, attempting to get out of the remains of the White House. With horror, you also notice that a column is swaying and is about to crash on to this poor soul. You, in your helicopter, have the means to lower a rope and save an individual from certain death. You have a decision to make. You can either take the shot, which will be the crowning of your career and be considered for decades by some as a work of art depicting human suffering and the quality of death in its highest, purest form. On the other hand, you can forget about fame, fortune and art and save your President.

When you have pondered this situation, please answer the following question as truthfully as you can:

Black and white, or colour?

DO KEEP UP

Osama bin Laden has sent another video to an Arab TV station in which he urges Muslims to go to holy war against America and the UK. He finishes by saying: 'I am alive and well. I am not a recluse who lives in fear and exile. To prove this, I can tell you that Liverpool were crap last Sunday.'

Government officials claim that this recording could have been made months ago.

GOD'S OWN COUNTRY

Press extract from Reuters: In a move that stunned opposition leaders, Prime Minister Tony Blair announced today that he was considering dropping what he called the 'regulations-infested quagmire of the European Union' in favour of the 'God-blessed bosom of Free America'. He then explained that Great Britain would be far more secure in its future as a nation if it rejoined the ranks of the other America states in the quest for 'status, political power and economic growth'.

In a speech that, to be fair, many political correspondents expected him to deliver at some point in his career, Tony Blair carried on by saying that the nation should open its eyes to the wealth of opportunities becoming the 51st State of America would provide.

'America is the last superpower on the planet. It would be sheer folly to overlook this fact and to pass on the chance of being, once again, part of something grander,' he concluded.

Answering astonished questions about the potential loss of traditional values such as the Royal Family, the British way of life and political integrity, the Prime Minister said: 'I have received assurances from President Bush that all the landmarks which constitute such a great country as ours will be preserved. England will remain England. We will not lose our identity as a nation: England with its rolling hills, its quiet churches and McDonald's restaurants, the England we all love and we all want to preserve and bring forward into the new millennium.'

Amid cries of consternation coming from backbenchers and members of the opposition as well, he explained that 'the American administration is ready to accept having the portrait of the Queen on dollar bills, which will have the same economic value as any other banknote: a value which is, I am sure my honourable friends will concede, very high indeed in today's world markets.'

He also remarked that this move towards an Americanisation of Great Britain was not something people should be afraid of. 'After all,' he concluded, 'we as a constitutional monarchy have always followed America's lead. This political move is just a ratification of what we have lived with for centuries without having the courage to accept. Now is the time to do it, now that we have already placed ourselves in the world's eye as a subsidiary of the United States anyway.'

NATURE'S MIRACLE

Apparently, the resting rate of President Bush's heartbeat is 43. Scientists are marvelling at how strange and wonderful it is to have a man whose heart rate matches his IQ.

CITIZEN SOLDIERS

This is the transcript of a directive coming from the MoD. This directive was leaked to one of our special correspondents.

RE: Shortage of Volunteers in the Armed Forces: It has come to our attention that the combined armed forces lack a fresh input of personnel. This situation is quite pervasive and could mean the United Kingdom might not be able to fulfil some of its economic and military goals in the colonisation of the Middle East.

In this light, it has become clear that the male population of Great Britain might need to be forcefully enlisted in order to boost army numbers.

This will not, of course, come without problems on its own, considering the chronic lack of resources from which the military suffers. Each new conscript will therefore be asked to contribute to their own kit, either by means of a bank loan or a mortgage. Allowances will have to be made for people with low or no revenues (the proximity to the line of fire should be proportional to income.)

The conscript will thus be encouraged to buy:

- Military uniform (khaki an advantage, but any sober colour will do. Please avoid pastel tone corduroys).

- Boots (Preferably steel toecap. Please, no trainers.)
- Canteen and rucksack.
- Helmet (please do not choose blue in colour, as this will interfere with the work of the UN).
- Transport. Soldiers will be eligible for special rates on Virgin Airways and Ryanair. Please note that re-routed Dover-Calais ferries will not stop on the continent for replenishing.
- Weapons. Please do not feel compelled to buy the latest weapon from your local arms dealer. If any weapon has come to you as a family heirloom – or if you live in Manchester – you can use your weapons if you so choose, as long as you can still find ammunition for them. Note also that all weapons must contain at least one moving part made of steel.

I SEE NO SHIPS

The Battle of Trafalgar in Blair's Britain, 2005

'Send the signal, Hardy.'

'I'm afraid I can't do that, Sir. Here are the new regulations regarding engagement.'

'New regulations? Let's have a look at them… mmmmmm… "England expects every person to do his duty, regardless of race, gender, sexual orientation, religious persuasion or disability." What's this?'

'Admiralty policy, I'm afraid, sir. We're an equal opportunities employer now. We had the devil's own job getting "England" past the censor. Also, we can't send up a flare, because they've been categorised as "display fireworks" and have to be used as part of a licensed public display.'

'Christ, Hardy! Hand me my pipe and tobacco.'

'Sorry, sir. All naval vessels have been designated smoke-free working environments.'

'In that case, break open the rum ration. It will give heart to the men before battle.'

'The rum ration has been abolished, Admiral. It's part of the Government's new "healthy living" policy.'

'Oh God, Hardy. I suppose we'd better get on with it. Order full sail.'

'I think you'll find that there's a 5km per hour speed limit in this stretch of water, sir. In any case, we can't go any faster, because we have 1,294 bureaucrats and managerial staff on board.'

'How many sailors do we have?'

'Seven.'

'I've had enough of this. Where's the midshipman?'

'Sadly, sir, the police found a penknife in his car during a random search. As he now has a criminal record, he had to resign his post.'

'Damn it, man... we are on the eve of the greatest sea battle in history! At the very least I want someone in the crow's nest.'

'That won't be possible, sir. Health and Safety have closed the crow's nest. There's no harness, and apparently the rope ladder doesn't meet European regulations. They won't let anyone up without a dayglo anorak and an orange helmet.'

'Then get the ship's carpenter to sort it out.'

'He's busy making a wheelchair ramp up to the upper deck, Admiral.

'We've been told to provide a barrier-free environment for the differently-abled. Unfortunately, the carpenter has only just got out of prison after being convicted for marking up wooden planks in Imperial measurements.'

'Well, tell the men to stand by to engage the enemy.'

'The men are starving, sir. All the ship's food has been impounded by environmental health officers as being three days past its 'consume by' date and too high in salt and saturated fats. The galley has been closed because of the possible presence of bacteria. The water supply has been dumped because it had one-millionth of a microgram per litre too much lead in it. Also, the gunners are a bit worried about firing the cannon.'

'What? But this is mutiny!'

'It's not that, sir. The thing is that the noise level would breach Directive 276986753457 and they're afraid of being charged with murder if they kill anyone. There's a couple of lawyers from the European Court of Human Rights on board, watching everyone like hawks. We've also had a very dispiriting signal. The BBC are saying that it is quite understandable for Napoleon to want to conquer all of Europe. *The Guardian* has a reporter in Paris saying that our sanctions are causing hardship. People with placards are demonstrating in London shouting "No to Trafalgar – not in our name". Kofi Annan says that we should negotiate.'

'Then how are we to sink the Frenchies?'

'We can't. According to the Common Fisheries Policy, we shouldn't even be in this area. We could get hit with a fine from the European Commission.'

'But... we must hate the Frenchman as we hate the devil...'

'I wouldn't let the ship's Diversity Sub-co-ordinator hear you saying that, sir. You'll be up on a disciplinary. We're supposed to be inclusive and multicultural. Now put on your Kevlar vest, it's regulations.'

'Oh dear. Whatever happened to rum, sodomy and the lash?'

'As I explained, sir, rum is off the menu and there's a ban on corporal punishment.'

'What about sodomy?'

'That's the one thing that the government is actively encouraging, sir.'

'In that case... kiss me, Hardy.'

Chapter 5
Celebrity jokes

SORRY, DAVE

What would be David Beckham's stage name if he was with the Spice Girls?
Waste of Spice.

ACADEMIC QUESTION

Celine Dion and Sir Cliff Richard are in a plane. The plane is crashing. Who will pick up the only parachute?
Who cares?

BREAST FRUIT FORWARD

If you were to throw a rotten tomato at Britney Spears on stage, it would give you a perfect D minor.

TRAGEDY

Around 1900, the famous Yugoslavian comic Izigonadoit Hedidit could blow out a candle with a fart at a distance of three metres. Then electricity replaced the candles and he died a pauper.

HEAVEN CAN WAIT

Luciano Pavarotti dies and goes to the Pearly Gates.

'And you claim to be Pavarotti?' asks Saint Peter.

'What do you mean, I claim to be Luciano Pavarotti? I *am* Luciano Pavarotti!'

'Well, you know how things are these days; everybody is trying to get into Heaven. You wouldn't *believe* to what lengths some people would go to come here. So I'll have to give you a test, I'm afraid. Can you sing 'O Sole Mio' for us?'

Luciano Pavarotti breathes in and sings a magnificent version of 'O Sole Mio'.

'It's OK, I do believe you are who you say you are,' says Saint Peter and the great tenor enters Heaven.

Elton John dies and arrives in front of the pearly gates. Saint Peter, explaining once again that people would do anything to get into Heaven, asks him to sing and prove he is Sir Elton.

Sir Elton agrees and sings a version of 'Candle in the Wind' that has the poor Saint Peter in tears. Sniffling, he opens the gates to heaven to Elton John.

Celine Dion dies and goes to see Saint Peter.

'My dear lady, I just had Pavarotti and Elton John recently and they had to prove to me they were who they said they were. Can you do the same?'

Celine looks at him blankly. 'Who?' she asks.

'It's OK; you can come in,' Saint Peter says with a sigh.

THAT'S MY BOY

Michael Jackson's wife has a baby. It has been a lengthy affair and the mother is exhausted. The singer, on the other hand, is over the moon.

'And how long should we wait before we can have sex?' he asks the doctor.

'Oh, you'll have to wait at least 12 years.'

PUT A TIGER IN YOUR TANK

Tiger Woods is at the wheel of his brand-new BMW in a remote corner of Ireland. He's been driving for miles and realises he's got to get some petrol. He drives for a few more miles and spots a rickety petrol station. He pulls over and an old geezer comes to the pump.

'Can you fill it up, please?'

The old guy shuffles to the pump and starts pumping. He eyes the car and says to Tiger Woods: 'That's a good-looking car you have here, mister. What make is it?'

'It's a BMW. They're made in Germany.'

The old guy nods. After a few minutes the tank is full and they go to the counter. Tiger takes his wallet out and some tees fall out of his pocket. The attendant has obviously never seen a tee, or heard of Tiger Woods, and asks: 'You dropped these, sir. What are they?'

'These are called tees. They're to rest my balls when I drive.'

The old guy hands them over to the golfer with respect. 'Those German engineers: they think of everything, don't they?'

AN AMERICAN TRAGEDY

Bill Gates: 'What did you do with the $200 million dollars I asked you to invest? I said Apple, not Snapple!'

COMPOSE YOURSELVES

A famous Hollywood film director has an idea for a movie. He wants to portray the life of renowned classical composers, with a twist. Instead of casting people like Hugh Grant or Johnny Depp, he'll use actors who are not usually associated with culture, such as Van Damme, Stallone and Schwarzenegger.

He phones them up in turn and asks them what they think about this idea.

'That's great,' Van Damme says. 'You know what? I've always admired Mozart. I would really like to drop my hard-guy, all-muscle image and play Mozart.'

The film director agrees to have him play Mozart and phones up Stallone.

'If I can, I'd like to play Chopin. I'm sure I'd be good at it. Thank you for thinking about me for this venture,' Stallone says.

Confident about the whole scheme, he phones up Arnie and explains the project to him. There is a moment of silence at the other end and then Arnie says: 'I'll be Bach.'

ON THE JOBS

'My girlfriend always laughs during sex – no matter what she's reading.'

Steve Jobs (Founder of Apple Computers).

SAD SONGS THEY SING

Stan Collymore and Sir Elton John are walking in the park one day when they come across a young woman. She's in a rather awkward position: apparently, she's bent over to pick up a flower on the lawn and stuck her face through the railing.

This is too good an opportunity to pass and Stan drops his shorts to take the young woman from behind. He enjoys himself immensely (and, we are led to believe, the young woman does too) and when he's finished, he turns to Sir Elton John.

'Would you like some of that?'

'No,' the singer answers. 'My head will never fit between these railings.'

ALL YOU EVER WANTED TO KNOW ABOUT SEX

Did you hear about Woody Allen's latest movie?

It's called: 'Honey, I Married the Kids.'

CHILLY WILLIS

What does Bruce Willis see when he goes skiing?

Icy dead people.

REMEMBER THIS ONE?

What happened when Batman and Robin got run over by a steam roller?

They became Flatman and Ribbon!

Chapter 6
Chav Jokes

'Chav' (slang) – a young person, often without a high level of education (and who's unlikely to achieve any in the near future), who follows a particular fashion;

Most likely to be wearing:

Male:

Chavs usually wear designer labels including Burberry. Chavs consider branded baseball caps as a symbol of their social status (the goods do not need to be genuine). They will often be seen with their tracksuit trousers tucked into their socks.

Female:

Very short skirts, large hoop earrings and stilettos or trainers without socks. All their clothes will stop at midriff and trousers at mid-calf.

Bad habits (both sexes):

Fast food. Alcohol (preferably alcopops). Cigarettes. Bubble gum.

Jewellery
Fake gold in large amounts. Very heavy chains with dollar signs or brands. Huge earrings for girls.

Normally found hanging around shopping centres, clinics, Spar shops, pizza places, around other pregnant 15-year-olds.

Also known as Townies, Kevs, Hood Rats, Charvers, Steeks, Stigs, Bazzas, Yarcos, Ratboys, Skangers, Scutters, Kappa Slappers, Scallies, Spides and, in Scotland, Neds.

Here is what a proud chavette would say:

> I think chavs are great, coz I is one, innit? There's nuffin wrong wiv Burberry & S.I. and I think Novas are pure class. When I'm cruisin round the mall all the other birds are well jealous cos they fink my choons are well bangin. My Dan reckons I am the fittest bird in school and none of the older girls can down Smirnoff ice like I can. I can drink 10 bottles and I'm only 15! One more thing: Goths are crap, innit?

The New Essex Dictionary

ASSA COMMONS – Our Parliament building.

ART ATTACK – Extremely perturbed, as in 'Don't tell Sharon, She'll have a art attack.'

ARST – Past tense of 'ask', as in: 'Jordan, I must of arst ya free fazzund times to clear up yer room.'

BANNSA – A person employed to deny access or eject troublemakers at a club. 'Dave's got izself a job as a Bannsa.'

BANTY – A chocolate and coconut snack bar.

BAVE – To wash oneself.

BOAF – The two. 'Oi Dave, ooja fancy most, Sharon or Tracy?' 'Boaf' is the reply.

BRANSATCH – Motor racing circuit in Kent.

CANCEL – Administrative body of a town. 'Darren, wive ad annuvva letter from the cancel.'

CANTAFIT – Fake, as in money.

CHOONA – An edible fish purchased in a tin and usually prepared with mayonnaise.

CORT A PANDA – A big hamburger (smaller than an arf panda)

DAN TO URF – Sensible, practical.

DANNING STREET – Where the Prime Minister lives.

DANSTEZ – On the ground floor, where the biggest telly is.

DREKKUN – Do you consider? as in 'Which dog drekkun'll win the next race?'

EFTY – Considerable. 'Ere, Trace, this credit card bill's a bit efty.'

EJOG – A small, spiky animal.

ERZ – Belonging to her.

EVVY – A big geezer who protects a smaller and more intelligent geezer, usually for money. 'My name's Frank and this is my evvy, Knuckles.'

EYEBROW – Cultured, intellectual.

FANTIN – A jet of water for drinking or ornament.

FARVA – A posh way of saying 'Dad'.

FATCHA – Margaret, British Prime Minister 1979 – 1990.

FINGY – A person or object whose name doesn't come to mind. 'I ad it off wiv fingy last night.'

FONG – Skimpy undergarment.

FOR CRYIN AT LAAD – Mild expletive showing annoyance or surprise, eg. 'For cryin at lad, Britney, if I say Yes will you give it a rest?'

GAWON – Go on. 'Gawon Darren, eat ya granny's cabbage, it'll do yer good.'

GIVE IT LARGE – To be thorough or enthusiastic.

GRAND – A football stadium. 'It all wennoff atside the pub near the grand.'

HAITCH – Letter of the alphabet between G and I.

IBEEFA – The Spanish holiday island.

IFFY – Dubious. 'Ere, Trace, I fink this bread pudding you made last munf's a bit iffy.'

INT – Indirect suggestion. ' I gave Darren a sort of int that it was time to wash iz feet.'

IPS – An unknown area of a woman's body to which chocolate travels. 'That Mars Bar will go straight to me ips.'

JA – Do you, did you. 'Ja like me new airdo, Sharon.'

JACKS – Five-pound note. 'Lend us a jacks, wilya?'

JAFTA – Is it really necessary? 'Oi mate, jafta keep doing that?'

KAF – Eating house open during the day.

KAFFY – A girl's name.

LAD – Noisy. 'Jordan, turn that music dan; it's too lad.'

LARJ – Enjoying oneself.

LEVVA – Material made from the skin of an animal.

LOTREE – Costs £1 for a ticket.

MA BLARCH – An arch near Hyde Park.

MAFFS – The study of numbers.

MANOR – Local area.

MINGER – An unattractive person (usually female).

NARRA – Lacking breadth, with little margin. 'Mum wannid to come rand but changed er mind. That was a narra rescape.'

NARTAMEAN – Do you know what I mean? (sometimes used as 'janartamean').

NEEVA – Not one nor the other.

NES – National Elf Service.

OAF – A solemn declaration of truth or committment.

OLLADAY – Time taken away from home for rest and adventure.

ONNIST – Fair and just; without a lie. 'I never did it, onnist.'

OPPIT – Go away , as in 'Oi you, oppit.'

PADDA PUFF – Soft, lacking aggression. 'They're all right up front but they got a padda puff defence.'

PACIFIC – Specific.

PAFFUL – Having much power or strength.

PAIPA – Sun, Mirror etc.

PANS AN ANNSIS – Imperial weights system.

PLAMMANS – A pub lunch usually made up of cheese and bread.

QUALIDEE – Good, as in 'West 'Am's new striker's qualidee.'

RAND – A number of drinks purchased for a group.

RANDEER – Locally. 'There ain't much call for it randeer.'

REBAND – Period of recovery after rejection by a lover. 'I couldn't 'elp it. I was on the reband from Craig.'

ROOFLESS – Without compassion.

SAFF – A direction of the compass, opposite north.

SAFFEND – An Essex seaside town.

SAWTED – Done, arranged, resolved.

SEEVIN – Very angry. 'I woz seevin when I urd wot 'e sed.'

TALENT – Attractive members of the opposite sex. 'Dave's gan dan tan to eye up the talent.'

TAN ASS – A modern terraced house.

TOP EVVY – A woman of plentiful bosom. 'Ere, look at that, Darren; she's well top evvy.'

UG – An unattractive person. 'Sharon's new geezer's a bit of an ug.'

UMP – Upset, as in 'Got the Ump'.

VACHER – A document which can be exchanged for goods or services. 'I got a vacher to get in cheap at Forp Park.'

WANNED UP – Tense. 'I'm all wanned up at the moment.'

WAWAZUT? – I beg your pardon?

WENNOFF – A fight commenced, as in 'It all wennoff'.

YAFTA – You must : 'Even if yer guilty, yafta av mitigating circumstances.'

YOOF OSTALL – A place where holidaymakers can stay the night.

ZAGGERATE – To suggest something is better or bigger than is true. 'Craig, I must've told ya a fazzund times already.' 'Don't zaggerate, mum.'

What do you call a chav in a filing cabinet?
Sorted.

What do you call a chav having sex?
Innit.

What do you call a chav who's got a date for the weekend?
Innit safe.

What do you call a chav in a white tracksuit?
All white.

What do you call an Eskimo chav?
Innuinnit.

Why are chavs like Slinkies?
They have no real use but it's great to watch one fall down a flight of stairs.

What do you call a chavette in a white tracksuit?
The bride.

If you see a chav on a bike, why should you try not to hit him?
It might be your bike.

What's the difference between a chav and a coconut?
One's thick and hairy, the other's a coconut.

What's the first question at a chav quiz night?
'What you lookin' at?'

How do you get 100 chavs into a phone box?
Paint three stripes on it.

Two chavs in a car without any music. Who's driving?
The police.

What do you say to a chav at work?
Can I have a Big Mac, please?

What do you call a large group of chavs descending on a pub?
A chavalanche

Where do you take a chavette for a decent night out?
Up the gary!

What do you call a chav in a boiler suit?
A prisoner.

What is a chav's favourite pastime?
Drinking cider at the bus stop.

What is a chav's short-term plan in life?
A three-month sentence.

What is a chavette's short-time plan in life?
I'd like to start the kids at school before I finish my GCSEs.

Why do chavs always travel around in pairs?
One can read and one can write!

What do you do if you run over a chav?
Reverse, just to make sure.

What do you call a chav in a dinner jacket?
Waiter!

What do you call a French chav in a dinner jacket?
Garçon!

What do you call a chav in the dock?
Guilty.

What do you call a chav at college?
The caretaker.

Where do chavettes go for work?
Street corners.

What do you call a pregnant chavette?
An underage mother.

Why are chavs like laxatives?
Because they irritate the shit out of you.

How do you save a chav from drowning?
Take your foot off his head.

ESSEX EDUCATION

How do you know Essex County Council chavs invented the female body?

Because only they would be stupid enough to put a play area next to a shithole.

IF MUSIC BE THE FOOD OF LOVE, FUCK OFF

A chav walks into a pub and puts some money in the jukebox. 'I'm not playing that shit! Now fuck off!' the jukebox shouts.

The bemused chav looks at the barman, who says: 'Yeah, that jukebox is really out of order'.

OBVIOUS EGGSPLANATION

Two chavs are riding double on an old motorbike. All of a sudden the engine splutters, coughs and dies. Here they are, stranded on the side of a road that is far from busy. They wait an hour before seeing a lorry. They try to hitchhike, but the driver, seeing they are chavs, just ignores them. Another hour passes and a less discerning lorry driver stops.

'Gis a ride, mate, innit?' one the chavs implores. 'We've just broke down.'

'Tell you what,' the driver says. 'I'm hauling bowling balls in my truck. There should be just enough room for you and your bike, guys.'

The lorry driver sends down the tailgate and pushes both the bike and the young chavs in.

On the way, he's stopped by the police for a routine check.

'What are you carrying in there?' the officer asks.

'Chav eggs,' the trucker replies.

'Chav eggs? You're pulling my leg.'

The officer opens the door to the trailer and, to his dismay, finds hundreds of bowling balls, a bike and two chavs. He rushes back to the car and yells through the radio: 'I need backup! I just stopped this lorry that's carrying chav eggs. Two of them have hatched and they've already had time to steal a motorbike!'

IN YOUR DREAMS

A chav walks into the job centre and says: 'I'd like a job, please.'

'Well, you've come to the right place! I think we have something for you… wait… yes, here it is: no qualifications required, part-time, £780 a week.'

The chav stares at him, hope stretching slowly across his pustulent face, and says: 'You're joking, right?'

'Hey – you started it!'

Chapter 7
Jokes from around the World

AS LONG AS HE'S HAPPY

A Hispanic family were considering putting their grandfather into a nursing home. All the Catholic facilities were completely full, so they had to put him into a Jewish home. After a few weeks in the Jewish facility, they came to visit grandpa.

'How do you like it here?' asked the grandson.

'It's wonderful! Everyone here is so courteous and respectful,' replied grandpa.

'We're so happy for you. We were worried that this was the wrong place for you.'

'Let me tell you about how wonderfully they treat the residents here,' grandpa says with a big smile. 'There's a musician here – he's 85 years old. He hasn't played the violin in 20 years and everyone still calls him 'Maestro'! And there's a physician here – 90 years old. He hasn't been practicing medicine for 25 years and everyone still calls him 'Doctor'!

'And me – I haven't had sex for 30 years and they still call me 'the fucking Mexican."

THE MYSTERIOUS ORIENT

An Italian, an Irishman and a Chinese are working together. The foreman, who is English, tells them: 'Right. See that pile of stones there? The Italian will dig it, the Irishman will clear it with the wheelbarrow and the Chinese will be in charge of supplies. Everyone agrees?' They all nod and off he goes for a pint.

He comes back an hour later. The Italian and the Irish are playing cards and the pile of stones hasn't diminished one bit.

'What's the meaning of this? Why aren't you working?' the foreman fumes.

'Well, where's my shovel?' the Italian asks.

'And where's my wheelbarrow?' the Irish guy asks.

'I don't understand; the Chinese guy was supposed to be in charge of supplies.'

'Well, we haven't seen him ever since you left, boss.'

Just at this moment, the Chinese guy jumps out from behind the pile of stones and jubilantly shouts: 'Supplies!'

WE'VE ALL BEEN THERE

How do you recognise a French woman at the hairdresser's?

She's the only one with rollers under her arms.

LAGER THAN LIFE

What is the difference between making love in a canoe and a can of cheap beer?

There isn't any: it's fucking close to water.

THIS SEPTIC ISLE

God has created earth and invites Michael the Archangel to have a look.

'Looks like another blue ball of stuff to me,' he says to God, depreciatingly.

'Ah, but wait! You see, I'm going to create life on this one,' God says proudly. 'I am also going to give this place balance. You see these two long stretches of land there? That will be North America and South America. One will be poor while the other will be wealthy.'

'I see,' the archangel says doubtfully. 'And what's there?'

'There? That will be Great Britain. It will be a fantastic place to live, full of exquisite lakes and majestic lochs. There will be beautiful coastlines and green hills. It will be a lush land with gentle rivers and apple trees.'

'Hold on: you were talking about balance a second ago,' remarks Michael.

'Yes, well, I'm gonna fill it with Englishmen, Welsh and Scots.'

WHO WAS THAT MASKED MAN? WHAT MASKED MAN?

One day, the Lone Ranger and his faithful friend Tonto were surrounded by hostile Indians. Negotiations had fallen through and the horde was ready to attack. The Lone Ranger turned to Tonto and said: 'My dear friend, what do we do?'

'What do you mean, what do *we* do, white man?' Tonto asked.

AND NOW... YOUR FIRST LIGHTBULB JOKE

How many Puerto Ricans does it take to change a lightbulb?

Juan.

A SLUR ON THE PROUD NAME OF ERIN

How do you recognise an Irishman in a car wash?

He's the one on the bike.

CHACUN A SON GOUT

A French and an English gynaecologist meet at a conference. The French guy says to his British counterpart: 'I recently treated this woman: she had a vagina like a melon.'

The British gynaecologist makes a face.

'You French – you're disgusting. How can you say the vagina of this poor woman was the size of a melon? How gross.'

'You British; always thinking about size. I was talking about the flavour.'

POLYMORPHOUS PERVERSITY

What is a very polite Greek?

A guy who's been going out for three weeks with a girl before asking her brother out.

THE MEDITERRANEAN LIFESTYLE

A Greek and an Italian were sitting down one day debating who had the superior culture.

The Greek says, 'We have the Parthenon.'

The Italian says, 'We have the Coliseum.'

The Greek says, 'We had great mathematicians.'

The Italian says, 'We had the Roman Empire.'

And so on and so on and so on, until the Greek man says: 'We mastered sex!'

So the Italian says, 'That's true; but it was the Italians who applied it to women.'

WE CAN TAKE IT

What is long and hard and aims at 55 million assholes?

The Channel Tunnel.

WIRELESS CONNECTIVITY

After having dug the soil for a month, British scientists discovered copper wire dating back 500 years, buried deep. They came to the conclusion that the British people already had a telephone exchange 500 years ago. Not to be outdone, the Americans started digging too and claimed they had found, buried at a depth of 600 metres, a network of fibre optic wire dating back 2,000 years which proved the American people had the Internet at the time Jesus was born. The Belgian government decided to have a go too. Their team of scientists dug and dug, but found nothing. The Belgian government therefore stated that the results of this experiment clearly showed that 2,000 years ago Belgians had mobile phones.

SNOTLAND THE BRAVE

Why do Scots have big noses?

Because they have big fingers.

OH, BAD LUCK

An Irish guy and a Scot end up in a pub. They spend a few minutes ogling the girls before they find a couple they'd like to talk to.

'Come on, Ben; let's chat them up!'

'Er... I don't know, Shaun. I'm not very good at chatting up girls.'

'That's not a problem. Just do as I do.'

The Irish guy approaches one of the beauties and asks her to choose a number between one and ten.

'Er... Five?'

'Congratulations! You've won a drink; what will you have?' and they leave together towards the bar.

The Scot is well impressed and decides to have a go:

'Give me a number between one and nine,' he says to the other girl.

'Er... Eight?' she replies with a smile.

'Damn. You lost,' the Scot mutters angrily.

WAITING IN VAIN

A Russian is walking the streets of Moscow when he stumbles upon a queue. He doesn't even think about it: he just stops behind the guy in front and waits. After an hour, the queue hasn't moved. Perplexed, he taps on the shoulder of the guy in front and asks: 'tell me, comrade; what are we queuing for?'

The guy stares at him, then confesses: 'I don't know. I just saw people waiting, so...' The other just nods in understanding. 'Hold on; I'll pass the question up.'

So the guy in front asks the woman in front, who asks the woman in front... and so forth. After another hour, the guy is quite surprised to see the queue in front of him dismantle. Everybody is leaving.

'What was that all about?' he asks the guy in front as he makes to depart.

'Oh, it was this woman,' he explains. 'she bent down to lace her shoes when someone stopped behind her. Then she thought, 'Well, for once I'm at the head of a queue: I'll just wait.'

AND WHY NOT?

Why do Swiss men wear three condoms?

So that the one in the middle remains clean.

BUM RAP

An Irish couple decides to go skiing in Scotland in winter. They've been there the previous year and had a great time, so they try to get a room at the same hotel.

Once there, they book the same room and go to the reception.

'We came here last year and had a fantastic time,' the wife says. 'We had a very friendly ski instructor who really helped us. Do you reckon we could book him again this year?'

'That shouldn't be a problem, Madam. What was his name?'

The couple look at one another. They rack their brains, but can't remember the guy's name.

'Well, do you have a description? What did he look like?'

'He was tall and tanned and was wearing a red jumper all the time,' the wife says.

'That's no great help, I'm afraid, the receptionist says with a laugh. 'We are a ski resort. The town is full of young tanned men with red jumpers. Do you remember anything else?'

They look at one another again, concentrating, when the man chuckles: 'Yes, there is a detail that might help.'

'What is it?'

'Well, I don't know if I should say it – it's kind of personal, I suppose – but this guy had two anuses.'

'Two anuses?' the receptionist exclaims, dumbfounded. 'How do you know that?'

'Well, we were skiing one day and another instructor came along and asked him: 'How are you doing with your two assholes?'

OVER-RUN

An American has pulverised the record for the 100 metres.

He's run 103 metres.

MOTHER TONGUE

What's long and hard and is given to a Russian woman when she gets married?

A new name.

LOCH AYE THE NOO

Why is it OK to let Scots drown?

Because deep down they're not that bad.

WIZARD WHEEZE

Baghdad is full of rats. It's terrible; they're everywhere, and the Iraqi authorities haven't managed to get rid of them. The Americans have tried gunning them down and frying them with napalm, to no avail: every time the rats come back. No one knows what to do.

An old Iraqi hears about their plight and tells them there's an old seer, somewhere in the desert, who it is said has a magic weapon against rats. The Iraqi officials scoff, but surreptitiously send a man out into the desert.

The guy indeed finds the old wizard and relates his people's plight.

'How can we get rid of the rats?'

'It is true, I have a cure for your rats. Here; take this

box. Go back to Baghdad and open it there. When the rats have gone, come back and return the box to me.'

The guy picks up the box and goes back home. Once in Baghdad, he opens the box and is quite surprised to see a green rat in it. The rat is like a normal, average rat, only it's all green. The rat looks at him with a knowing smile and is off. Soon all the rats follow him. They come from everywhere: the old presidential palace, what's left of the sewers, the new barracks... they all follow the green rat, who leads them into the desert, where they all die.

It's a miracle. The guy picks up the green rat, puts it back in the box and goes back into the desert to thank the old wizard.

'Here's your rat,' he tells him. 'Now, tell me; you wouldn't have a green American by any chance?'

HARD AT IT

An Italian under-secretary to a minister, anxious to be promoted, asks his colleague: 'Tell me, how many people are working under your supervision?'

'Oh, I'd say two out of ten.'

ALL RIGHT ON PAPER

An English couple move into a flat next to an American couple. They make friends and invite one another for a drink at regular intervals. One evening, at one of their monthly reunions, the British couple notice that the American couple have changed the wallpaper of their flat.

'It looks very nice,' the English wife congratulates them.

'And he did it himself, too!' exclaims the American wife, obviously proud of her husband's skills.

Back in their own flat, the British couple decide it's time for them to change the wallpaper as well. A week later, the husband goes next door and asks: 'Where did you get your wallpaper from? You see, I've got to redecorate now,' he says with a smile.

The American guy says: 'I got it from Homebase. I bought 11 rolls.'

Seeing that their flats are identical, the British bloke buys 11 rolls of wallpaper from Homebase. When the redecorating is done, they invite their American friends over.

'Good job,' the American wife tells them. 'Looks very cool!'

'Yeah, but I can't understand why I've got four rolls left,' the British husband says.

'Yeah, I've got four rolls left too,' the American guy says, baffled.

SANDWICH

What is a Russian sandwich?

A ham voucher between two bread vouchers.

NOT SO BIG NOW, ARE WE?

George W Bush has a problem. The factory which makes most of America's condoms has inexplicably stopped working. All he can do to make sure the population of the States enjoy safe sex is to phone up the Belgian Foreign Minister.

'Allo, Pierre? I have un probleme. Il faut des condoms.'

'No problem, Mister President. We'll just increase our home production to accommodate your needs.'

'Send me 10 million condoms. But be careful: they need to be blue, red and white and be 40 centimetres long.'

The Belgian Prime Minister thinks that these Americans really like to boast and that this demand is quite ridiculous, but he agrees nonetheless. With alacrity, he phones up the condom factory.

'The American government has placed an order for 10 million condoms,' he says to the guy in charge of production.

'10 million? That will stretch our resources, but we can do it.'

'He wants them blue, red and white.'

'That's not a problem whatsoever, Minister.'

'One last thing: they need to be 40 centimetres long.'

The guy at the other end burst out laughing.

'40 centimetres? Who do they think they are?'

'I know, I know, but they're paying, so we've got to deliver. Only, I'd like you to do me a favour: print on each and every one of them 'Made in Belgium. Size: Small'.

TAKE A DEEP BREATH

Why do Scots REALLY have big noses?

Because oxygen is free.

SMART THINKING

Why do Scots wear kilts?

Because the sound of a zip frightens the sheep.

SMALL WORLD

An American is staying in a hotel in Paris. He's been going on about how everything in France is small. He complains that the Champs Elysées are nothing compared to the Strip in Las Vegas, that the Arc de Triomphe pales compared to the George Washington Monument and so forth. In short, he makes a pest of himself and thoroughly annoys the staff with his stupid comments. The American tourist carries on slagging off the French about how small their country is to such an extent that a chambermaid decides to take her revenge. She goes to his room and places a live lobster in the offensive guy's bed.

The American tourist finally stops talking and goes to his room. A few minutes later, the chambermaid hears a scream and witnesses him rushing out and slamming the door behind him.

'What's the matter, sir?' she asks him.

'There's a huge… thing in my bed!'

'O, I am so sorry, sir. It is so hard to get rid of bedbugs,' she says airily.

MORE TOILET HUMOUR

Shaun is ill. He goes to see his GP, who prescribes a suppository.

'You take this via the rectum,' he tells him.

Shaun acquiesces, although he doesn't have a clue what a rectum is. Puzzled, he goes and sees a friend.

'Say, do you know what a rectum is?'

'Nope.'

After two hours spent driving around his friends asking

the same question – and getting the same answer – Shaun gives up and goes back home. He gets a glass of water and simply swallows the damn pill.

It takes him a while to get better. Two weeks later, he goes back to his GP.

'So, did you see any improvement with your treatment?'

'Aw, no,' Shaun says. 'It didn't work. I could have shoved this pill right up my ass and it wouldn't have been any better!'

A SIGN OF THE TIMES

At the Quebec-Canada border, there are two factories.

On the Quebec side, there is a sign that says: 'Here, we speak French.'

On the Canadian side, there is also a sign, but it says: 'Here, we don't talk; we do some work.'

MAMMARY LAPSE

Why do French women have small breasts with big nipples?

Because Frenchmen have small hands but have a big mouth.

THEY'RE SO PHYSICAL

How do you shut up an Italian?

You just have to tie his arms behind his back.

THEY GET YOU EVERY WAY

Three Russians have been sent to the gulag.

'I had to go to this committee meeting and I arrived 15 minutes late,' the first one says. 'I was accused of being a saboteur and here I am.'

'I had to go to a meeting too and I arrived 15 minutes early, so here I am,' says the second Russian.

'I had to chair a meeting, so I arrived on time,' the third one says. 'So they said I had bought my watch in the West and here I am.'

A QUICK DASH ROUND THE SHOPS

A Russian lady goes to the butcher's.

'Good morning, comrade butcher. Do you have any bread?'

'Ah, you're making a mistake, dear lady,' the butcher retorts. 'Here we don't have any meat.'

REFRESHES THE PARTS

A Dutchman, from the deepest part of the Dutch countryside, ends up one day in Amsterdam. He's heard of Amsterdam. He's heard, in particular, of the red light district, where prostitutes offer the lot: rental of the hotel room, a shag and a pack of beer. He decides to go and have a look.

The first prostitute he meets says that the lot is £250. That's far too expensive for him. Unfortunately, prices in a great city are high but, after a couple of hours' bartering, he finally meets an old decrepit whore who tells him that the lot is only £25.

'I have to warn you, though,' she says. 'I don't have a clitoris.'

'Oh, it's OK with me,' replies the guy. 'I'll have a Heineken.'

NIGHTMARE SCENARIO

A plane crashes on an isolated island in the middle of the Pacific Ocean. Only a few people make it: there are Italians, Germans, French, Swiss, Russians, British, Greeks, Swedish and Irish. Unfortunately, there are two men and only one woman of each nationality. After a week:

One Italian man has killed the other to get the Italian woman.

The two German guys enjoy the company of the German girl on a weekly basis in strict rotation.

The two French men and the French woman live together in a harmonious ménage à trois.

The two Swiss men cordon off a section of the island and declare themselves neutral.

The two Russian men have a good look at the Russian woman and decide to try to swim to shore.

The two British guys patiently wait for someone to introduce them to the British lady.

The two Greek men live together while the woman does the dishes.

The two Swedes discuss the virtues of suicide at length while the woman goes to the beach naked.

The two Irish blokes promptly divide the island in two and build a distillery in the middle, thinking that sex is not important as long as the British don't get any.

CASHBACK

Two Irish guys and an English bloke end up in a strip joint together. The evening is young and they have a few beers: then the first stripper starts pole-dancing. She approaches them and wriggles her butt in the face of the first Irish guy, who takes a tenner out of his wallet to place it in the stripper's thong. She smiles at him and moves her butt to the next Irish guy, who does exactly the same. Lastly, she moves on to the English guy and dances seductively at him. The guy opens his wallet, takes out his credit card, swipes it through the stripper's crack and picks up the two tenners.

HEAVY PETTING

What do you call a guy in Shropshire who's carrying a cat and a dog?

A bisexual.

The two Welsh [illegible] while the woman goes to the [illegible] naked.

The two Irish blokes [illegible] divide the island into two and [illegible] [illegible] don't get any.

[illegible]

Two [illegible] end up in a [illegible] [illegible] have [illegible] the first [illegible]

[illegible] the face of the [illegible] to place [illegible] the same. [illegible]

[illegible] [illegible] the two [illegible]

[illegible]

What do you call a [illegible]

[illegible] a badge [illegible]

[illegible]

[illegible] a [illegible] [illegible] [illegible]

Chapter 8
Silly jokes

BE PREPARED

A company of Girl Guides is moving silently through the forest, as part of an exercise. They have been walking for a couple of hours when they hear muffled sounds in the distance. As they approach the source of these noises, it becomes clear to the lady in command that what is ahead should not be seen by her charges. She holds up her hand and says: 'Stop! I think there's a dangerous beast ahead.' It is too late, though. Through a clearing in the wood, the girls plainly see that what is making these noises is a man and a woman performing some kind of naked activity. They seem to be having a great time doing it. One of the girls says in an awed tone: 'Wow: I know what merit badge I'm going to go for next.'

OH, THE SHAME

A renowned doctor is talking to a friend at home over a glass of wine. His little girl comes in and, obviously bored, picks up her dad's stethoscope.

'See?' he tells his friend proudly. 'She wants to follow in my footsteps!'

The little girl, oblivious, picks up the wrong end of the stethoscope and speaks into it: 'Welcome to McDonald's. May I take your order?'

OUR LITTLE MIRACLE

The boss of a big company needs to call one of his employees about an urgent problem with one of the main computers. He dials the employee's home phone number and is greeted with a child's whispered 'Hello?'

Feeling put out at the inconvenience of having to talk to a youngster, the boss asks, 'Is your Daddy home?'

'Yes', whispers the small voice.

'May I talk to him?' the man asks.

To the boss' surprise, the small voice whispers, 'No.'

Wanting to talk to an adult, the boss asks, 'Is your Mummy there?'

'Yes', comes the answer.

'May I talk to her?'

Again the small voice whispers, 'No'.

Knowing it is unlikely that a young child would be left home alone, the boss decides just to leave a message with the person who should be there watching over the child.

'Is there anyone there besides you?' he asks.

'Yes,' whispers the child, 'a policeman.'

Wondering what on earth a policeman is doing at his employee's house, he says, 'and can I talk to this policeman?'

'No: he's busy talking to Mummy and Daddy and the fireman, too.'

The boss is growing quite worried when the conversation is drowned out by a deep rumbling sound.

'What was that noise?' he asks the child.

'The search team's helicopter just landed,' the small voice whispers back.

'A search team? What for? What are they looking for?' the boss cries, alarmed.

'Me,' giggles the little voice.

HOUSEHOLD HINTS

How do you sanitise nipples?

Bathe daily and wear a clean bra. It beats boiling them in a saucepan.

OOPS

A wife says to her husband: 'The kids are growing up and we'll have to be careful when we make love. I spoke to Gladys next door and she told me that little John asked them some pretty awkward questions when he found a condom in the conservatory.'

At this moment Anna, a little girl with big ears, comes in and asks: 'Mum, what's a conservatory?'

GEE, THANKS

A man goes to see a counsellor.

'Tell me; we've just had a baby and my wife's behaving strangely. Do you have a clue when she'll be acting normally again?'

'Oh, when your kid's at university, I expect,' the counsellor replies.

WELL PUT

School is boring, especially today, when the lesson is about the proper use of vocabulary. The teacher has asked everyone to think about a sentence using the word 'beautiful' twice, but little Billy can't be bothered.

First, she asks Mary, who responds with: 'My father bought my mother a beautiful dress and she looked beautiful in it.'

'Very good, Mary,' replied the teacher. 'Joe, can you give me a sentence using the word "beautiful" twice?'

Joe makes a face, concentrates and ends up with: 'My dad bought a beautiful tree for Christmas and we all put beautiful decorations on it.'

'Well done!' the teacher congratulates Joe. 'What about you, Billy?'

'Last night, at the dinner table, my sister told my father that she was pregnant and he said, "Beautiful; just fucking beautiful!"'

FASTER THAN A SPEEDING BULLET

Ray loves roleplay. His mum has made him a beautiful red cape and he can spend hours pretending he's Superman. He can rush down the stairs making whooshing noises pretending to fly; he can flatten empty cornflake boxes as a show of strength… He's been having so much fun with this cape that he decides to hide it in his bag for his first day at school.

Once at school the following day, Ray goes to the toilet and gets changed into his Superman gear. The teacher, who's seen it all and who knows that little boys sometimes need the reassurance of familiar objects and clothes when they first start school, says nothing when he sees Ray wearing his outfit.

At registration, however, the teacher comes across a problem. He's approached Ray with a form for him to fill in and asked his name. Ray, obviously, has replied 'Superman.'

'That's a good joke,' the teacher says. 'Now I need your real name, to put on your form, you see?'

'Superman,' Ray repeats.

'OK, that was funny the first time, but now we need to get cracking,' the teacher says, thinking that he's got 30 kids to go through before break time. 'Now, tell me your *real* name, please.'

Seeing that the teacher is not amused, Ray leans forward. 'All right, I'll give you my *real* name,' he whispers in his ear in a confidential voice. 'My *real* name is Clark Kent. Don't go and tell anyone else, OK?'

STOPPING AT TWO

A little boy is off on a walk with his hcavily pregnant mum. On the way they meet one of her friends she hasn't seen for a while and the friend marvels at her nice, big, round belly. She turns to the little boy and asks: 'Are you excited about having a little sister or brother soon?'

'Oh, yes!' he replies, his eyes bright. 'I even know what we're going to call them!'

His mum makes a show of surprise and nods for him to continue.

'I heard them say, "If it's a girl, we'll call her Sophie. If it's another boy, we'll call it quits."'

THAT'S WHAT I CALL TEACHING

On her school report, little Ann's teacher has written the following:

'Ann is a very good pupil. She's very smart and very enthusiastic. She has achieved all the goals that we set together last term. There is still a little bit of a problem with her talking too much, but I have an idea as to how to remedy that.'

Ann's dad, after reading the report, sends back the following comment: 'I'm glad to see that Ann is making good progress at school. I am also glad you might have found a way to stop her from talking all the time. If your idea works, could you share it with me so that I can try it out with her mum?'

GRUB'S UP

At school, the kids are asked to think about hygiene. The teacher has devised a little roleplay exercise and has asked her pupils to think about what their parents say at the table when they share food.

'My mum always says to go and wash my hands,' little Suzy says.

'That's good,' the teacher says. 'You should always wash your hands before eating, so that you don't get germs and microbes into your food.' She looks at the forest of raised hands and picks another pupil.

'My mum always says to me not to play with my food,' little Bob says.

'Correct,' the teacher congratulates Bob. 'If you play

with your food, you might drop it or you might not chew correctly.'

She notices that little Tim didn't raise his hand. She knows he is a bit shy. Wanting to push him a bit to interact with the rest of the group, she asks him; 'What about you, Tim? What do your parents say before you eat?'

'Order something cheap,' Tim replies, his eyes downcast.

FATAL SUBTRACTION

The maths teacher asks Harry a question: 'If there are five birds sitting on a fence and you kill one with your rifle, how many birds will there be left?'

Harry thinks for a minute and then says: 'Well, I kill one, but all the other birds will be afraid and fly off, so I guess the answer is zero.'

'Well, the correct answer is four, but I like the way you're thinking!' the teacher laughs.

Harry, who doesn't like being made fun of, decides to get the teacher back. 'OK; I have a question for you, then. There are three women sitting on a bench. One is reading the paper, one is working on her laptop and one is licking an ice-cream cone. Which woman is married?'

'Well,' the teacher answers, sensing something wrong but not really knowing what it is. 'The one licking an ice-cream cone?'

'Nope. It's the one with a ring on her finger. But I like the way you're thinking.'

DOLLY LOLLY

It's Christmas, and a man wants to buy a Barbie doll for his daughter. He goes to the toy shop.

'I'd like a Barbie for my daughter,' he says to the assistant. 'Do you have any?'

'Oh, yes: we have the entire Barbie collection here. Barbie Goes to School for £45, Barbie Goes to Church for £42.50, Barbie and her favourite pony for £75, Pop Star Barbie at £60 and Divorced Barbie at £3,500.'

'£3,500? How come this one is much more expensive than the rest?'

'Well, it comes with Ken's house, Ken's car, Ken's furniture and Ken's boat…'

LOG CABIN TO WHITE HOUSE

'Daddy, when I grow up, I want to be President of the United States!'

'Son, you can't have both.'

IT'S FOR THE BEST

A six-year-old boy is talking to his dad about his plans for the future: he and little Mary next door are going to get married.

'Is that so?' the dad asks. 'And where are you going to live?'

'We'll just go and live in the tree house.'

'I see. That's an interesting concept. What about money to get food?'

'We'll just pool our pocket money and we should have enough to get food,' the boy replies.

The dad decides to play the game to the end, so he asks: 'What if you have children? They cost a lot of money, you know.'

'Mary and I've talked about it,' he replies in the most sensible tone. 'Mary has agreed that if she ever lays an egg, we'll stomp on it.'

COARSEWORK

Little Harry comes back from school with a bad report in arithmetic. This is a surprise for his dad for, while Harry couldn't be called a brilliant student, he usually gets good marks in arithmetic.

'What happened?' he asks his son.

'The teacher asked me what six times three was.'

'What did you say?'

'I said 18.'

'That's the right answer,' his dad agrees.

'Then she asked me what three times six was.'

'Three times six or six times three: what's the fucking difference?'

'That's what I said too,' replies little Harry.

TOP MARKS FOR EFFORT

The teacher asks little Vicky to try to use the word 'disappointment' in a sentence. She wants to broaden her pupils' vocabulary and she often gives them quick surprise exercises like this.

Little Vicky is at a loss. She thinks hard for a minute and then she smiles broadly.

'I know! I heard mum say this once: "I'm sorry, doctor, but the traffic made me late for disappointment."'

IN GOD WE TRUST

Little Johnny is at the beach and he has a problem. He looks around and notices a matronly lady sitting underneath a parasol. He approaches her and says: 'Lady, are you a Christian?'

The woman pats the cross hanging between her voluminous breasts and replies: 'Yes, I am.'

'And do you believe that God will punish you if you do something wrong?'

'I certainly do.'

'And do you go to church often?'

'I go to church every day,' she replies proudly.

'Good. Could you keep an eye on my bag while I go swimming?'

PEW WHAT A SCORCHER

A Sunday school teacher asks her little charges, as they're on the way to the church service: 'Why do we have to be quiet in church?'

One bright little girl replies: 'Because people are sleeping.'

TRAIN STRAIN

A little boy is playing with his train set. His mum can hear him from the kitchen, making sounds and inventing dialogues.

'Liverpool Street Station! Get your ass in gear and get into the train!'

His mum freezes while drying the dishes, but lets it pass.

'Paddington Station! Come on, assholes, you're gonna miss the train!'

This time the mum is sure she's heard correctly, so she goes to the living room and warns her son: 'Joe, I want you to stop talking this way. Stop swearing: it's not nice!'

The boy shrugs, the mum goes back to the kitchen and a few minutes later she hears: 'Victoria Station! The first half of the train is for Shit-Brain City only!'

This is too much for the mum and she grabs her son by the ear and drags him up to his bedroom. She keeps him in there for a couple of hours and then relents, hoping he's understood the lesson.

The boy comes back down, powers up his train and shouts: 'Charing Cross! Two-hour delay because of a bitch on the tracks!'

LET IT BEE

It is the time of life when a father has to explain certain things to his children, so Dad takes his son aside one day and asks him: 'Tim, do you know about the birds and the bees?'

The boy stares at him and suddenly bursts into tears. The dad, not expecting this kind of reaction, is flabbergasted.

'What's the matter, poppet?'

'When I was six, you told me that Santa Claus didn't exist. You did the same thing a year later with the Tooth Fairy. Please don't tell me that when I grow up I won't get laid!'

DOMESTIC SILENCE

A little boy has managed to land a part in the school play. He's very proud of this and tells his father.

'That's grand,' Dad congratulates his son. 'What part is it?'

'I'm playing the part of the husband. He's been married to this woman for 25 years.'

'Really good!' replies the dad. 'Remember that this is just the beginning of your thespian career. Maybe next time you'll get a speaking part.'

WRONG-FOOTED

A kindergarten teacher is helping this little boy to put his boots on. He needs some help and she soon sees why: they're very tight indeed. After 15 minutes of pushing and pulling, she manages to fit the boots on the little boy's feet, when he says: 'They're on the wrong feet.'

Groaning, the teacher checks – and, indeed, she's done it wrong. She spends another 15 minutes taking them off and another 15 putting them back on the right feet.

'These aren't my boots,' the little boy says. The teacher takes a deep breath, ready to scream something along the lines of, 'Why didn't you say so before, you moron?', but she bites her tongue and remains silent. She struggles to take the boots off and asks where his own boots are. The little boy points innocently at the pair of boots she's just taken off and says in a serious tone; 'They're my brother's boots. My mum couldn't find mine this morning, so she made me wear these ones.'

The teacher is close to tears. With a mighty effort of

will, she refrains from hurling the damn boots across the room and instead she puts them back on the little boy. It takes a while, but at last he is ready to go out. The teacher is dishevelled and sweaty. Her arms and shoulders ache.

'Right. We're done with the boots. Where are your mittens?'

'I packed them at the bottom of my boots.'

Chapter 9

Men vs. Women jokes

DARLING, YOU'VE MADE MY DAY

One day a man came home and was greeted by his wife dressed in a very sexy nightie. 'Tie me up,' she purred, 'and you can do anything you want.'

So he tied her up and went golfing.

HARSH... BUT TRUE

What do you call a woman who has lost 95 per cent of her intelligence?

Divorced.

UP, UP AND AWAY

Aeroplanes are better than women because...

Aeroplanes can kill you quickly – women take their time

Aeroplanes can be turned on by the flick of a switch

Aeroplanes don't object to a pre-flight inspection

Aeroplanes come with manuals to explain their operation

Aeroplanes have strict weight and balance limits

Aeroplanes can be flown at any time of the month

Aeroplanes don't come with in-laws

Aeroplanes don't care how many aeroplanes you've flown before

Aeroplanes and pilots both arrive at the same time

Aeroplanes don't mind if you look at other aeroplanes

Aeroplanes don't mind if you buy aeroplane magazines

Aeroplanes expect to be tied down

Aeroplanes don't comment on your piloting skills

Aeroplanes don't whine unless something is seriously wrong. However, when aeroplanes go quiet, just like a woman, it's a bad sign.

SO THAT'S IT

Scientists have discovered a food that diminishes a woman's sex drive by 90 per cent. It's called a wedding cake.

SLIPPERY CUSTOMER

A husband comes home with a tube of KY jelly and says, 'This will make you happy tonight.' He was right. When he goes out of the bedroom, his wife squirts it all over the doorknobs. He couldn't get back in.

STILL GETTIN' IT ON

One night an old lady comes home from bingo to find her 92 year-old-husband in bed with another woman. She becomes violent and ends up pushing him off the balcony of their 20th-floor assisted living apartment, killing him instantly. Brought before the court on a charge of murder, she is asked by the judge if she has anything to say in her own defence.

'Yes, Your Honour: I figured that at 92, if he could have sex, he could fly.'

COMMUNICATION BREAKDOWN

A virile young Italian gentleman is relaxing at his favourite bar in Rome when he manages to attract a spectacular young blonde. Things progress to the point where he invites her back to his apartment, and after some small talk, they retire to his bedroom and make love.

After a pleasant interlude, he asks with a smile, 'So...you finish?'

She pauses for a second, frowns and replies, 'No.'

Surprised, the young man reaches for her again and the lovemaking resumes. This time she thrashes about wildly and there are screams of passion. The lovemaking ends, and again, the young man smiles, and again he asks, 'You finish?' And again, after a short pause, she returns his smile, cuddles closer to him, and softly says, 'No.'

Stunned, but damned if this woman is going to outlast him, the young man reaches for the woman again. Using the last of his strength, he barely manages it, but they climax simultaneously, screaming, bucking, clawing and ripping the bed sheets. The exhausted man falls on to his back, gasping. Barely able to turn his head, he looks into her eyes, smiles proudly, and asks again, 'You finish?'

Barely able to speak, she whispers in his ear, 'No! I Danish.'

BATTLE OF THE SEXES

A family is sitting around the supper table. The son asks his father, 'Dad, how many kind of breast are there?'

The father answers, 'Well, son, there are three kinds of breasts. In her twenties a woman's breasts are like melons: round and firm. In her thirties to forties they're like pears: still nice, but hanging a bit. After 50, they're like onions.'

'Onions?'

'Yes: you see them and they make you cry'.

This infuriated the wife and daughter so the daughter said, 'Mum, how many kind of penises are there?'

The mother smiles, and looks at her husband and answers,

'Well, dear; a man goes through three phases. In his twenties, his penis is like an oak: mighty and hard. In his thirties and forties, it is like a birch: flexible but reliable. After his fifties, it's like a Christmas tree.'

'A Christmas tree?'

'Yes: dead from the root up and the balls are there for decoration only!'

I'LL SEE YOU DEAD FIRST

A couple are driving down a small country lane when the wife takes a deep breath and says: 'Honey, we've been married for a long time, but I'm having an affair and I want a divorce.'

The husband remains silent, but he increases his speed to 60.

'As I've been investing a lot in it, I want to sell the house so that I can buy a new one and livc with my new lover,' she carries on, emboldened by her husband's silence. His speed now is 70.

'I'm a mother and I couldn't stand being parted from the kids, so I've decided I'll have the kids too.'

The husband clenches his teeth and reaches 80.

'You're not saying anything. I know you feel angry and bitter, but it's for the best. Is there anything you want to keep? I'm willing to negotiate.'

The man finally breaks his silence just as he reaches 90, and a sharp bend in the road.

'Nah: I've got everything I need. I've got the airbag.'

SELECTIVE DEAFNESS

What women say:

'This place is a mess! C'mon,
You're a real slob: it's not going to go on like this, you and me!

Your stuff is lying on the floor
and you'll have no clothes
to wear at work tomorrow
get your ass off of this sofa right now!'

What men hear:

blah, blah, blah, blah, C'MON
blah, blah, blah, blah, YOU AND ME
blah, blah, blah, blah, ON THE FLOOR
blah, blah, blah, blah, NO CLOTHES
blah, blah, blah, blah, RIGHT NOW

HEY, GOOD LOOKING

A man is sprawled on the sofa, quietly reading the paper, when his wife bursts into the room.

'What happened to us?' She wails. 'You don't love me anymore; you don't pay any attention to me like you used to!'

'Yes, I do,' the husband says in a placating tone.

'Oh yeah?'" retorts the wife with heavy sarcasm. 'Show me that you still pay attention to me then. I am wearing something new today, try and guess what it is.'

The man sighs inwardly and says: 'You're wearing a new top.'

'No! This is a jumper I bought two years ago. I was wearing it at our wedding anniversary last year.'

'Mmmm... Let me think... You've changed your hairstyle!'

'No! I have been going to the same hairdresser for the last five years and haven't changed a thing to my hair!'

'Alright, I give up!' the husband shouts, annoyed by this silly game. 'I confess I have no idea what is different with you today. What is it?'

'I'm wearing a gas mask!' the wife screams.

YOU SILVER-TONGUED CAVALIER, YOU

There's this man who's very shy. Because he's very shy, he's never been out with a woman. He's finally found one he really, really wants to go out with, but he doesn't know how to go about it. He's managed to ask her to the restaurant, but now he's stuck. He knows he's going to clam up and be hopelessly shy for his date and he'll flunk it. In desperation, he goes to a friend for advice.

'Simple,' says his friend. 'Talk to her. I've always found that if you confine yourself to just a few questions, it's quite easy to start a conversation. Try these: talk about her family, then about food and – well, ask her a very deep, meaningful question: something psychological, maybe.'

Full of hope, his heart beating fast, he goes to his date: and here he is, sitting in front of the woman he loves, tongue-tied. With an enormous effort, he asks: 'Er... Do you have a brother?'

'No.'

Damn. He doesn't have a brother either, so the conversation ends rather abruptly. Floundering, he goes back to the bowl of soup he's ordered for starters and thinks fast. Finally, he comes up with a question that fits the second piece of advice his friend has given him.

'Do you like broccoli?'

'No.'

Blown it again. Full of resolve, but feeling inside that he's already failed to impress the lady, he finally asks: 'If you had a brother, do you think you'd like broccoli?'

DID YOU GET HEALED?

A woman goes to her local holistic healer: she's had a nasty problem that no conventional doctor has ever been able to cure.

'Honey, I have great news!' she tells her husband when she gets back home.

'Are you healed?' He asks.

'Not yet, but the healer said that all I need to do is to have sex every day for a month and my problem will disappear!'

'OK, I see,' the man muses. 'Book me in for a Saturday morning will you?'

THAT'S REAL LOVE

A new study of women has produced the following results:

85 per cent of women think their ass has grown too big since getting married. 10 per cent of women think their ass is just as big as it was when they got married. The other five per cent say they don't care; they love him and would have married him anyway.

VIVE LA DIFFERENCE

A French language teacher is trying to explain that French nouns are either masculine or feminine. She further explains that there's no grammatical rule to determine what gender a particular word is: a plate is feminine while a glass is masculine, and that's the way it is. To prove this, she divides the class into two groups, one male and one female, and asks the groups to find reasons why the noun 'computer' should be either masculine or feminine.

The group of women concludes that computers should be referred to in the masculine gender because:

In order to get their attention, you have to turn them on.

They have a lot of data but are still clueless.

They are supposed to help you solve your problems, but half the time they *are* the problem.

As soon as you commit to one, you realise that, if you'd waited a little longer, you might have had a better model.

The men, on the other hand, decide that computers should definitely be referred to in the feminine gender because:

No one but their creator understands their internal logic.

The native language they use to communicate with other computers is incomprehensible to everyone else.

Even your smallest mistakes are stored in long-term memory for later retrieval.

As soon as you make a commitment to one, you find yourself spending half your pay cheque on accessories for it.

I NEED SOME SPACE

There's a new book out to help couples achieve a better relationship. It's called, *Women Are From Venus, Men Are Wrong.*

WORK IT OUT

A guy finishes work early. He goes back home and finds his wife cleaning the kitchen floor. She's not wearing any panties and there she is, on all fours… He can't help himself, and seizes this golden opportunity by the hips. He has a good time and, after he is done, he slaps his wife on her bare buttocks.

'Hey! That hurt!' The wife complains. 'Here I am, making your fantasies come true and the only way you can think of thanking me is to slap me on the arse?'

'Yeah,' the husband replies angrily. 'You didn't even turn around to see who it was!'

WHAT EVERY WOMAN KNOWS

What women understand that men don't:

Cats' facial expressions

The need for the same style of shoes in different colours

Spending £50 on a hair cut that lasts two weeks

Why beansprouts aren't just weeds

Total control over eyebrows

The inaccuracy of every bathroom scale ever made

Taking a car trip without trying to beat your best time

Spending three hours in the bath

The difference between beige, off-white and eggshell

Eyelash curlers

Other women

YOU CRACK ME UP

A couple have a car crash. They are both OK, except that the wife ends up with a nasty scar on her cheek. The only thing doctors can suggest is plastic surgery. Unfortunately, there are few places on the body that match the smoothness and grain of the face. One of these places is the buttocks but, understandably, the woman is rather reluctant to have any skin removed from her bottom to be grafted on to her face: she doesn't really want to have a scarred bottom any more than she is prepared to accept a scarred face.

'Don't worry, honey,' her husband says. 'I'll donate some skin from my bum. I don't mind: I wouldn't like you to have a scarred bottom either; I love your bottom as it is too much for that.'

The wife is ecstatic, and can't believe that her husband will sacrifice his body for her.

The operation goes ahead as planned and, after a few weeks, the wife's face is once again smooth and beautiful. A year passes and they go out to celebrate the day they survived the terrible accident.

'Darling, I'm so proud of you. I don't know what to do to repay you for what you did for me,' she says over a glass of wine in a fancy restaurant.

'It's OK, honey: I get all the reward I need every time your mother kisses you on the cheeks.'

TAKE IT EASY, MAN

A man is enjoying his holiday. He's done nothing. He's managed to ignore the subtle hints from his wife to repair the leaking gutter, wash the car or apply a coat of paint to the garage, but always in such a crafty way that his wife can't actually complain. The hints become broader and more desperate, but still he manages to put off doing any chores until, one day, the washing machine breaks down and a cupboard door in the kitchen collapses simultaneously. She picks up the vacuum cleaner from underneath the stairs and starts vacuuming the sitting room, avoiding her husband's feet on the rug, when the hoover splutters, hiccups and dies. She stands still for a few seconds, then throws herself on the sofa, weeping uncontrollably.

'It's OK, honey; I'm here,' her husband says, making soothing noises. 'When all else fails, you still have me.'

'Yeah, but you don't work either,' she wails.

SIMPLE BUT EFFECTIVE

How do you get a man to do sit-ups?

Put the remote control between his toes.

YOU KNOW IT'S TRUE

How we use cash dispensers

Male procedure:

Drive up to cash machine.

Wind down your car window.

Insert card into machine and enter PIN.

Enter amount of cash required and withdraw.

Retrieve card, cash and receipt.

Wind up window.

Drive off.

Female procedure:

Drive up to cash machine.

Reverse the distance required to align car window with machine.

Restart stalled engine.

Wind down the window.

Find handbag, remove all contents on to passenger seat to locate card.

Locate make-up bag and check make-up in rear-view mirror.

Get out of car.

Get back into car and place everything back in handbag.

Get out of the car.

Quickly check make-up in side mirror.

Place left hand above eyes to read the screen. Check left hand fingernails.

Insert card.

Reinsert card the right way up.

Open handbag to find diary with the PIN written on the inside back page.
Enter PIN.
Press Cancel and re-enter correct PIN.
Enter amount of cash required.
Check make-up on screen.
Retrieve cash and receipt.
Empty handbag again to locate purse and put cash inside.
Place receipt in back of chequebook.
Re-check make-up.
Get back into car.
Walk back to cash machine and retrieve card.
Re-check make-up.
Start car.
Avoid accident when pulling out.
Restart stalled engine and pull out.
Drive for 3-4 miles.
Release handbrake.

SOMEBODY UP THERE LIKES ME

'My wife's an angel.'

'Lucky you. Mine's still alive.'

FINGERJOBS

A group of friends are having a few drinks in a posh bar. They talk about this and that and, after a few G&Ts, the conversation turns towards sex.

'A man is totally driven by his sexual needs,' a guy says.

'This is the reason why men get more pleasure from sex than women.'

Of course the women in the group disagree and it goes on like that for ten minutes before one of the women says to the guy: 'OK, I am going to ask you a question. Imagine your ear is itching. So you put your finger in your ear, right? Now tell me, what is feeling better afterwards? Your ear or your finger?'

YOU KNOW, THAT'S A VERY GOOD QUESTION...

If all brides are beautiful, where do ugly wives come from?

DOWN, BOY

Two friends are having a drink in a bar and, after a little while, the conversation turned to sex (as it usually does when two men are left together for too long).

'You're happy with your wife? Mine won't let me take her doggie style. Does yours?'

'Well, she *does* do a kind of doggie trick, yeah,' his friend replies.

'What do you mean, a kind of doggie trick? Kinky stuff?'

'Not really... it's more the "roll over, play dead" kind of trick she does.'

AND WHY NOT?

If men got pregnant:

Maternity leave would last two years with full pay.

There would be a cure for stretchmarks.

Natural childbirth would become obsolete.

Morning sickness would rank as the nation's No. 1 health problem.

All methods of birth control would be 100 per cent effective.

Children would be kept in the hospital until toilet-trained.

Men would be eager to talk about commitment.

They wouldn't think twins were so cute.

Sons would be home from dates by 10pm.

Briefcases would be used as nappy bags.

Paternity suits would be a fashion line of clothes.

They'd stay in bed during the entire pregnancy.

Restaurants would include pickles and ice cream as their main starters.

NOT SHAGGING: SAGGING

A man says to his wife after ten years of marriage: 'You're getting old. You've got wrinkles now.'

The wife is incensed and yells: 'They're not wrinkles; they're laughter lines.'

'Come on; nothing's that funny.'

HUMAN CHEMISTRY

Element Name: WOMAN

Symbol: WO

Atomic Mass: Accepted as 118lbs., known to vary from 110 to 550lbs.

Physical properties:

Surface usually covered with chemicals of various hues.

Boils at nothing, freezes without reason.

Melts when given special treatment.

Bitter if incorrectly used.

Found in states varying from virgin metal to common ore.

Yields to pressure applied at correct points.

Chemical properties:

Has an affinity for gold, silver, platinum and precious stones.

Absorbs great quantities of attention.

Extremely volatile and may explode without warning for no apparent reason.

Insoluble in water, but activity greatly increased with alcohol.

Most common uses:

Primarily ornamental, especially in sports cars.

Found to be a great aid to relaxation.

Tests to carry out to check purity:

Genuine specimens will leak at first contact.

Pure specimen turns rosy pink when discovered in its natural state.

Turns green when placed next to a fresher specimen.

Hazards:

Hard to retain when left in inexperienced hands.

Illegal (not to mention deadly) to use more than one specimen at a time.

Element Name: MAN

Symbol: XY

Atomic Mass: 180 lbs. +/- 50

Physical properties:

Solid at room temperature, but gets bent out of shape easily.

Fairly dense and sometimes flaky. Difficult to find a pure sample. Due to rust, ageing samples are unable to conduct electricity as easily as young samples.

Chemical properties:

Attempts to bond with WO any chance it can get. Also tends to form strong bonds with itself. Becomes explosive when mixed with Kd (Element: Child) for prolonged period of time. Neutralise by dousing with alcohol.

***Usage*:**

None known. Possibly good methane source. Good samples are able to produce large quantities on command.

Caution: In the absence of WO, this element rapidly decomposes and begins to smell.

YOU NEED TO KNOW THIS

What women say and what they really mean:

I need: *I want.*

We need: *I want.*

It's your decision: *The correct decision should be obvious by now.*

Do whatever you want: *You're going to pay for this later.*

We need to talk: *I need to complain.*

Sure...go ahead: *I don't want you to.*

I'm not upset: *Of course I'm upset, you moron!*

You're so manly: *You need a shave and you sweat a lot.*

You're certainly attentive tonight: *Is sex all you ever think about?*

I'm not emotional! And I'm not overreacting!: *I have a severe case of PMT.*

Be romantic; turn out the lights: *I have flabby thighs.*

This kitchen is so inconvenient: *I want a new house.*

I want new curtains: *I want new curtains, new carpeting, new furniture, new wallpaper...*

I need new shoes: *the other 40 pairs are simply the wrong shade.*

I heard a noise: *I noticed you were almost asleep.*

Do you love me?: *I'm going to ask for something expensive.*

How much do you love me?: *I did something today you're really going to hate.*

I'll be ready in a minute: *Kick off your shoes and find a good game on TV.*

Is my butt fat?: *Tell me I'm beautiful.*

You have to learn to communicate: *Just agree with me.*

Are you listening to me?: *Too late; you're dead.*

Yes: *No.*

No: *No.*

Maybe: *No.*

I'm sorry: *You'll be sorry.*

I was wrong: *Not as wrong as you.*

Do you like this recipe?: *It's easy to make, so you'd better get used to it.*

Was that the baby?: *Why don't you get out of bed and walk him until he goes to sleep?*

I'm not yelling!: *Of course I'm yelling; this is important!*

What men say and what they really mean:

I'm hungry: *I'm hungry.*

I'm tired: *I'm tired.*

Do you want to go to a movie?: *I'd eventually like to have sex with you.*

Can I take you out to dinner?: *I'd eventually like to have sex with you.*

Would you like to dance?: *I'd eventually like to have sex with you.*

Can I call you sometime?: *I'd eventually like to have sex with you.*

Nice dress!: *Nice cleavage!*

You look tense; let me give you a massage: *I want to fondle you.*

What's wrong?: *What meaningless self-inflicted psycho trauma are you going through now?*

You look upset: *I guess sex tonight is out of the question.*

Yes, I love your new hairstyle: *I liked it better before.*

Yes, your haircut looks good: *£50 and it doesn't even look different!*

I liked the first dress you tried on better: *Pick any bloody dress and let's go!*

AND THAT'S HOW WE LIKE IT

A man has six items in his bathroom: a toothbrush, toothpaste, shaving cream, a razor, a bar of soap and a towel from the Holiday Inn. The average number of items in the typical woman's bathroom is 337. A man would not be able to identify most of these items.

POOR PUSSY

Women love cats.

Men say they love cats, but when women aren't looking, men kick cats.

FOR ONCE, NO CHICKENS

Why did the woman cross the road?

Who cares? What the fuck was the bitch doing out of the kitchen?

WISE ADVICE

If you ever wanted to be a bigamist, think again: you'll have two mothers-in-law.

RUDE AWAKENING

Every Wednesday morning for the past three years Harry has woken up early, got his breakfast and headed off to the nearest lake for a whole day of fishing. This Wednesday, however, the weather is just too bad. He's used to being cold and doesn't mind the wind, but today it would actually be dangerous for him to go out. As he walks out to his car in the drive, he realises that he's got to give up.

Silently he comes back in and shakes off his soaking coat in the kitchen. He quietly sneaks back into the bedroom and, once there, he gets undressed and climbs into bed.

'Oh, hello, John,' his wife says sleepily. 'I didn't know if you'd come this morning with this weather. Would you believe my moron of a husband went fishing in this rain?'

WELL, NOW YOU DO

I married Miss Right. I just didn't know her first name was Always.

TAKE IT EASY, LADY

Signs that you are having PMT:

Everyone around you has an attitude problem.

You add chocolate chips to your cheese omelette.

The dryer has shrunk every last pair of your jeans.

Your husband is suddenly agreeing with everything you say.

You're using your mobile phone to dial up every bumper sticker that reads, 'How's my driving? Call 0845 xxx xxx.'

Everyone's head looks like an invitation to batting practice.

You're convinced there's a God and he's male.

You're counting down the days until the menopause.

You're sure that everyone is scheming to drive you crazy.

The ibuprofen bottle is empty and you bought it yesterday.

Three little letters (M, E, and N) send you into an uncontrollable rage.

GET USED TO IT

Three couples are in a restaurant. Two couples have been married for only a short while: the others have been together for years.

The first wife says to her husband: 'Could you pass me the sugar, sugar?'

The man gives her a look of total infatuation and passes the sugar.

'Could you pass me the honey, honey?' said the second wife. The husband smiles and it's like the sun is setting in his eyes.

The last woman looks at both the young wives in a way a teacher would look at a particularly slow student and says: 'Can you pass me the bacon, pig?'

THAT'S GRATITUDE FOR YOU

A woman's husband has been slipping in and out of a coma for several months, yet she stays by his bedside every single day. One day he comes to and motions for her to come nearer.

She leans in, and he says, 'You know what? You've been with me all through the bad times. When I got fired, you were there to support me. When my business failed, you were there. When I got shot, you were by my side. When we lost the house, you gave me support. When my health started failing, you were still by my side... You know what?'

'What, dear?' she asks gently.

'I think you bring me bad luck.'

AND THAT'S WHERE IT ALL STARTED TO GO WRONG

'God,' said Adam, 'why did you make Eve so beautiful?'

'So you would love her.'

'But why did you make her so dumb?'

'So she would love you.'

GET THIS DOWN

For all you guys out there who just can't figure it out, here it is: In the world of romance, one single rule applies: Make the woman happy. Do something she likes and you get points. Do something she dislikes and points are subtracted. You don't get any points for doing something she expects. Sorry: that's the way the game is played. Here is a guide to the points system.

Simple Duties:

You do the washing up: 0

You do the washing up, but don't clean the sink: 0

You don't put the clean dishes away but leave them to dry: -1

You don't clean the greasy frying pans: -5

You clean the toilet: 0

You don't clean under the seat: -5

You leave the toilet lid up: -10

You replace the toilet-paper roll when it's empty: 0

When the toilet-paper roll is bare, you resort to paper hankies: -1

When the paper hankies run out, you shuffle slowly to the next bathroom: -2

You go out to buy her spring-fresh extra-light panty liners with wings: +5

But return with beer: -5

You check out a suspicious noise at night: 0

You check out a suspicious noise and it's nothing: 0

You check out a suspicious noise and it's something: +5

You trash it with a baseball bat: +10

It's her father: -10

Social Engagements:

You stay by her side during the entire party: 0

You stay by her side for a while, then leave to chat with a college drinking buddy: -2

Named Naomi: -4

Naomi is a dancer: -6

Naomi has implants: -8

Her Birthday:

You take her out to dinner: 0

You take her out to dinner and it's not McDonald's: +1

It is McDonald's: -2

It's in a restaurant at an all-you-can-eat night: -3

It's a pub with live sport, it's all-you-can-eat night with free beer and your face is painted in the colours of your favourite team: -10

A Night Out With The Boys:

Go out with a pal: -5

And the pal is happily married: -2

Or frighteningly single: -7

And he drives a convertible: -10

With a personalised numberplate (GR8 N BED): -15

A Night Out:

You take her to a movie: +2

You take her to a movie she likes: +4

You take her to a movie you hate: +6

You take her to a movie you like: -2

It's called Sudden Death 3: -3

Which features cyborgs having sex: -9

You lied and said it was a foreign film about orphans: -15

Your Physique:

You develop a noticeable pot-belly: -15

You develop a noticeable pot-belly and exercise to get rid of it: +10

You develop a noticeable pot-belly and resort to loose jeans and baggy Hawaiian shirts: -30

You say, 'I don't give a damn because you have one too': -800

The Big Question:

She asks, 'Do I look fat?'

You say 'No': 0

You hesitate in responding: -10

You reply, 'Where?': -35

Communication:

When she wants to talk about a problem, you listen, displaying what looks like a concerned expression: 0

When she wants to talk, you listen for more than 30 minutes: +5

You listen for more than 30 minutes without looking at the TV: +10

She realises this is because you've fallen asleep: -20

A PHILOSOPHICAL QUESTION

If a man says something in the woods and no woman hears him, is he still wrong?

A FREAK OF NATURE

A woman gives birth and afterwards the doctor comes into the room and says, 'I have something to tell you about your child...'

The woman slowly sits up with a worried look on her face and says, 'What's wrong with it?'

The doctor says, 'There's nothing really wrong with it, it's just a little different! It's a hermaphrodite.'

The woman looks confused. 'A hermaphrodite? What's that?'

The doctor replies, 'It has features of both a male and a female.'

The woman looks relieved. 'What? You mean it has a penis AND a brain?'

POWER OF THE PRESS

A man inserts an ad in the classifieds: 'Wife wanted'. The next day he receives 100 letters all saying the same thing: 'You can have mine.'

THAT'LL TEACH YOU

I never knew what real happiness was until I got married; and then it was too late.

AIN'T IT THE TRUTH?

Marriage is the triumph of imagination over intelligence.

Second marriage is the triumph of hope over experience.

CAN'T ARGUE WITH THAT ONE

My girlfriend told me I should be more affectionate. So I got two girlfriends.

MARK THE CALENDAR

The most effective way to remember your wife's birthday is to forget it once.

MISTAKES YOU ONLY MAKE ONCE

Words to live by: Do not argue with a spouse who is packing your parachute.

EVOLUTION NEVER LIES

Why do women have smaller feet than men?

So they can stand closer to the kitchen sink.

HELL ON EARTH

One Sunday morning, everyone in the bright, beautiful, tiny town gets up early and goes to the local church. Before the service, the townspeople are sitting in their pews and talking about their lives, their families, etc. when suddenly Satan appears at the front of the church. Everyone starts screaming and running for the door, trampling one other in a frantic effort to get away from evil incarnate. Soon everyone is evacuated from the church, except for one elderly gentleman who sits calmly in his pew, not moving... seemingly oblivious to the fact that he is in the presence of God's ultimate enemy.

Now, this confuses Satan a bit, so he walks up to the man and says, 'Don't you know who I am?'

The man replies, 'Yep: sure do.'

Satan asks, 'Aren't you afraid of me?'

'Nope; sure ain't,' says the man.

Satan is a little perturbed at this and asks, 'Why aren't you afraid of me?'

The man calmly replies, 'Been married to your sister for over 48 years.'

THE RULES

1. A man will pay £20 for a £10 item he wants. A woman will pay £10 for a £20 item that she doesn't want, then will take it back the following week.
2. A woman worries about the future until she gets a husband. A man never worries about the future until he gets a wife.
3. A successful man is one who makes more money than his wife can spend. A successful woman is one who can find such a man.
4. To be happy with a man you must understand him a lot and love him a little. To be happy with a woman you must love her a lot and not try to understand her at all.
5. Married men live longer than single men – but married men are a lot more willing to die.
6. Any married man should forget his mistakes – there's no use in two people remembering the same thing.
7. Men wake up as good-looking as they went to bed. Women somehow deteriorate during the night.

8. A woman marries a man expecting he will change, but he doesn't. A man marries a woman expecting that she won't change and she does.
9. A woman has the last word in any argument. Anything a man says after that is the beginning of a new argument.
10. There are two times when a man doesn't understand a woman: before marriage and after marriage.

KIDS THESE DAYS

It's the spring of 1957 and Bobby goes to pick up his date. He's a pretty hip guy with his own car. When he goes to the front door, the girl's father answers and invites him in. 'Carrie's not ready yet. Why don't you have a seat?'

Carrie's father asks Bobby what they're planning to do. Bobby replies politely that they will probably just go to the soda shop or a movie.

'Why don't you two go out and screw? I hear all the kids are doing it!'

Naturally, this comes as a quite a surprise to Bobby, so he asks Carrie's dad to please repeat himself.

'Yeah,' says Carrie's father, 'Carrie really likes to screw; she'll screw all night if we let her!'

A few minutes later, Carrie comes downstairs in her little poodle skirt and announces that she's ready to go. Almost breathless with anticipation, Bobby escorts his date out of the front door.

About 20 minutes later, Carrie rushes back into the house, slams the door behind her and screams at her father: 'Dad, it's called the Twist!'

WHEN YOU GOTTA GO...

A woman accompanies her husband to the doctor's surgery.

After his check-up, the doctor calls the wife into his consulting room alone and says, 'Your husband is suffering from a very severe stress disorder. If you don't do what I'm about to tell you, your husband will surely die.

'Each morning, fix him a healthy breakfast. Be pleasant at all times. For lunch, make him a nutritious meal. For dinner, prepare an especially nice meal for him. Don't burden him with chores. Don't discuss your problems with him: it will only make his stress worse. No nagging. And most importantly, make love with your husband several times a week. If you can do this for the next ten months to a year, I think your husband will regain his health completely.'

On the way home, the husband asks his wife. 'What did the doctor say?'

'He said you're going to die,' she replies.

CLEARING THE SHELVES

For sale: Complete set of Encyclopaedia Britannica. No longer needed: wife knows everything.

THE TRUTH AT LAST

Top 10 female rejection lines (translated)

10. I think of you as a brother. *Translation*: You remind me of that inbred, banjo-playing geek in 'Deliverance'.

9. There's a slight difference in our ages. *Translation*: I don't want to do my dad.
8. I'm not attracted to you in 'that' way. *Translation*: You are the ugliest dork I've ever laid eyes on.
7. My life is too complicated right now. *Translation*: I don't want you spending the whole night or else you may hear phone calls from all the other guys I'm seeing.
6. I've got a boyfriend. *Translation*: I prefer my male cat and a half-gallon of Ben and Jerry's.
5. I don't date men where I work. *Translation*: I wouldn't date you if you were in the same solar system, much less the same building.
4. It's not you; it's me. *Translation*: It's you.
3. I'm concentrating on my career. *Translation*: Even something as boring and unfulfilling as my job is better than dating you.
2. I'm celibate. *Translation*: I swore I wouldn't go out with men like you.
1. Let's be friends. *Translation*: I want you to stay around so I can tell you in excruciating detail about all the other men I meet and have sex with. It's the male perspective thing.

Top 10 male rejection lines (translated)

10. I think of you as a sister. *Translation*: You're ugly.
9. There's a slight difference in our ages. *Translation*: You're ugly.
8. I'm not attracted to you in 'that' way. *Translation*: You're ugly.
7. My life is too complicated right now. *Translation*: You're ugly.
6. I've got a girlfriend. *Translation*: You're ugly.

5. I don't date women where I work. *Translation*: You're ugly.
4. It's not you, it's me. *Translation*: You're ugly.
3. I'm concentrating on my career. *Translation*: You're ugly.
2. I'm celibate. *Translation*: You're ugly.
1. Let's be friends. *Translation*: You're sinfully ugly.

PROBABLY NOT A GOOD IDEA, THEN

I'm thinking about getting married. I looked up the word 'engaged' in the dictionary. It said, 'To do battle with the enemy.' Then I looked up mother-in-law. It said, 'See "engaged."'

NOT THAT KIND OF BUNK-UP

A man and a woman end up having to share a sleeping car, thanks to the unfathomable powers of the Virgin Trains booking system. They do not know one another and are quite shy at first, but after a while a kind of consensus is found: the man is going to sleep on the top bunk, while the woman is going to sleep at the bottom.

All goes well: they are snugly lying in their separate beds when the man says: 'Excuse me, miss, but can you reach the drawer where they keep the extra blankets? I'd do it myself, but I didn't want to disturb you by climbing down.'

The woman, who is just starting to fall asleep, wakes up with a start. She grumbles, but eventually gets out of bed and passes the guy an extra blanket. She goes back to sleep, only to be woken up a few minutes later.

'Excuse me; it's me again,' the guy says rather lamely. 'Could you pass me another pillow from the same cupboard?'

The woman takes a deep breath and replies: 'I'll tell you what. Seeing that we're getting on quite well together and we've got to share this car together, why don't we act as if we were actually together, like husband and wife?'

'Sure; that'd be great,' the man agrees, a sudden vision of acrobatic sex flashing through his mind.

'Good,' the woman purrs. Then she yells: 'Now get your lazy ass down and get your fucking pillow yourself, asshole!'

KILLING ME SOFTLY WITH HIS PONG

This being an old-fashioned couple, they haven't had sex before marriage. They get married pure and clean, as it were, and now is the time for the husband to panic. 'This is it,' he thinks. 'There's no turning back. I have to tell her now that I have a problem with my feet. They stink horribly. What am I going to do? I can't make love to her with my shoes on…'

As it happened, his young wife also had a problem. 'How am I going to explain to him that I have very bad breath at night? I know this isn't really a problem during the daytime, when I can go and wash my mouth every hour, but at night? He'll want to have sex in the middle of the night and so will I. What am I going to do?'

They both conceal their secret fears on the way to the honeymoon suite. It's quite late and they've had a few drinks. The husband lays his bride on the bed and says: 'Honey, I have a confession to make.'

'Me too, love.'

The husband makes a face and exclaims: 'I know: don't tell me. You've eaten my socks!'

HARSH BUT FAIR

A husband is whatever is left of the lover after all the nerve has been extracted.

Chapter 10
Naughty jokes

TAKEN SHORT

A man comes back home early one day and finds his wife in bed with a dwarf.

'How can you? You said you'd never cheat on me!'

'Well, I'm getting used to it little by little.'

STRAIGHT TALKING

A man enters a bar and orders a treble whisky.

'You must have had a rough day', the barman says to him sympathetically.

'Yeah. I just learned my younger brother's gay.'

He swallows down his drinks forlornly and leaves. The following day he's back and again orders a treble whisky.

'You again? What is it this time?'

'I just learned that my eldest brother is gay,' he replies and drinks up.

The following day he's back again and once again orders a treble whisky.

'Come on, man!' the barman exclaims. 'Isn't there

anyone in your family who likes women?'

'Yeah: my wife,' replies the man.

AH, BLESS

Why do women fake orgasms?

They think men care.

WE COME IN PEACE

Two lovers are on a walk one night, as a prelude to more athletic exercises later on in the evening. Things heat up a bit, though, and they end up in a bush lying on the man's coat when suddenly a harsh light catches them in an undignified position. The light is from an alien ship which has silently landed in a neighbouring field. Human-looking creatures emerge from the starship while the lovers frantically scramble to get their clothes back on.

'Please, do not be afraid, humans,' one of the aliens says in a strange voice coming out of his forehead. 'And please don't bother about your clothes. In fact, we've landed on Earth to study your species in general and your reproductive habits in particular. You've just given us an insight into how it is done and you will be rewarded now.'

Suddenly a ray of light shoots from the ship to the spot the couple have occupied a few minutes earlier and an impressive pile of gold ingots materialises out of thin air.

'Thanks to our matter transmitter, we can transform microwave particles into any solid matter we choose. Is this a fitting reward for your help?'

At a loss as to how to answer such a question, the man dumbly nods.

'We would appreciate it if you could help us further in our studies,' the alien carried on. 'We would like to compare your mating processes with ours. You would be duly rewarded again, of course.'

The lovers look at one another and discuss the offer for a bit. 'But honey, I love you.' 'We could be wealthy beyond our dreams!' 'I won't let them hurt you…' After a little while, they agree and climb into the spaceship, where they are led to separate cabins.

A couple of hours later, they are beamed out next to an even bigger pile of gold ingots and the spaceship departs. There is a long moment of awkward silence, and then the man asks: 'So, how was it for you?'

The woman looks at him, blushes and blurts out: 'It was the best sex I ever had. This guy had the most amazing penis. At first it was quite small; then I tugged on his left ear and it grew to the size of a big salami. I could make it as big or as small as I wanted.'

'I see,' the guy replies, then muses, 'That's why this alien woman spent two hours trying to pull my ears off my head.'

NEVER TRUST A…

A punk boards a bus and sits down next to a nun. Feeling mischievous, he leans over and asks her if she would like to have sex with him. Horrified, the nun bolts at the next stop.

'You know,' the bus driver then says to the punk, 'if you really want to do the nun, all you have to do is to turn up at the cemetery. She's there praying every night. Disguise yourself as God and order her to do it.'

The punk thinks it over and decides to have some fun.

Night falls and, true to the bus driver's prediction, the nun is there, praying over a grave. The punk passes a bed sheet over his head, fastens a false beard and goes over to her.

'Sister,' he says in a booming, God-like voice. 'I have taken human form to show you what sex is like so that you can better understand how to fight this evil in the world!'

The nun is cowed and bends her head.

'Your will, Oh Lord,' she whispers, 'but could we do it from behind, so I don't get pregnant?'

God agrees and soon they're at it like rabbits.

When the punk is finished, he takes off his bed sheet and his false beard and shouts: 'Surprise! It's not God, it's the punk!'

The nun turns around and takes her robe off, saying: 'Surprise! It's not the nun, it's the bus driver!'

LOGICAL EXPLANATION

A couple have just had a baby. The world would be a wonderful place but for one thing: they're both fair-skinned and have dark hair while the baby has freckles and red hair. They go to the GP and get some tests done.

'Well, I don't understand,' the doctor says. 'Let me reassure you: the tests are positive. You are both the parents of this child. There doesn't seem to have been any 'funny business', if you see what I mean. I don't really understand what happened there. Do you have any relatives with red hair?'

They both answer 'No' to the question, which makes

the doctor scratch his head in puzzlement. He turns to the husband and asks: 'Tell me, how often do you have sexual intercourse with your wife? Every day?'

'Man, no!' the guy says.

'OK, then: every week?'

'Er… no.'

'Every month?'

'No.'

'Every six months?'

'Yeah; that's about right,' the husband replies.

'I've got it now. It's just rust!'

TYPES OF SEX (1): SOCIAL SECURITY SEX

Two men are talking.

'So, how's your sex life?'

'Oh, nothing special. I'm having Social Security sex.'

'Social Security sex?'

'Yeah, you know: I get a little each month, but not enough to live on.'

TYPES OF SEX (2): LOUD SEX

A wife goes to see a therapist and says, 'I've got a big problem, doctor. Every time we're in bed and my husband climaxes, he lets out this ear-splitting yell.'

'My dear,' the shrink says, 'that's completely natural. I don't see what the problem is.'

'The problem is it wakes me up!'

TYPES OF SEX (3): QUIET SEX

Tired of a listless sex life, a husband comes right out and asks his wife during lovemaking, 'How come you never tell me when you have an orgasm?'

'You're never here!'

TYPES OF SEX (4): CONFOUNDED SEX

A man is in a terrible accident, and his manhood is mangled and torn from his body. His doctor assures him that modern medicine can give him back his virile member, but that his insurance won't cover the surgery since it's considered cosmetic. The cost will be $3,500 for a small one, $6,500 for medium and $14,000 for large.

The man's sure he wants medium or large, but the doctor urges him to talk it over with his wife before he makes any decision.

The man calls his wife and explains the options. When the doctor comes back into the room, he finds the man looking dejected.

'Well, what have the two of you decided?' asks the doctor.

The man answers, 'She'd rather have a new kitchen'.

FAT CHANCE

The Christmas holidays have come and gone and this guy decides to lose some of the weight he's gained throughout the festive season. He doesn't really want to go to the gym, though, so he's attracted by a little note in his local phone directory: 'Lose weight and have fun. Guaranteed.'

He phones up and makes an appointment. The following day, he drives to the address mentioned in the ad and rings the bell. He's quite surprised to be greeted by a sumptuous-looking brunette with inviting eyes.

'This way, sir.'

He is ushered into a beautifully furnished room, with plush armchairs and sweet music. He sits down in one of the seats and waits. After a little while, the woman enters the room and begins undressing. When she's naked, she grabs the guy's tie and purrs: 'If you can catch me, you can have me.'

There follows an hour of running around trying to catch this beautiful woman. He jumps over the furniture, he rolls and sprints, to no avail: she's much fitter than he is and evades him easily.

At the end of the hour, the woman stops and says to him: 'That will do for today. I guess you've lost quite a few pounds already. If you like this method, maybe you can come back in a week?'

The guy is beaming. Never has losing weight been that much fun. He eagerly gives his money and signs up for an appointment for the following week.

The following week, and the week after that, he chases the naked woman around. He's becoming much fitter and nearly manages to grab her on a couple of occasions.

Three weeks pass, and the man has a plan. He jogs to his appointment and as soon as he is ushered into the room, he gets undressed and starts rearranging the furniture, so that nothing gets in his way. Today is the day when he's gonna get this woman and have some *real* fun. The door opens... but instead of the beautiful naked lady is a huge man, naked apart from a loincloth.

'You are now entering the next stage of your training to lose weight,' he says to the puzzled guy. 'The rules are going to change slightly: now it's your turn to run, or I get *you.*'

OH DEAR

A gynaecologist says to his patient with a wide smile on his face:

'Well, Mrs Jones, I have great news for you...'

'It's not Mrs; it's Miss'

'Oh: sorry. As I was saying, I have bad news...'

DEAR JOHN

The manager of a large office noticed a new man one day and told him to come into his office. 'What's your name?' was the first thing the manager asked the new guy. 'John,' the new guy replied. The manager scowled, 'Look, I don't know what kind of a namby-pamby place you worked at before, but I don't call anyone by their first name. It breeds familiarity and that leads to a breakdown in authority. I refer to my employees by their last name only: Smith, Jones, Baker – that's all. I am to be referred to only as Mr. Robertson. Now that we've got that straight, what's your last name? The new guy sighed, 'Darling. My name's John Darling.' 'Okay, John, the next thing I want to tell you is...'

HE'S GOT A FLAT

Mary's husband is coming home with a tyre under each arm.

'What are you doing with these tyres? You can't even drive!' says Mary.

'So what? What about you? You buy bras, don't you?'

EUROPEAN UNION

A man is sitting in a train compartment opposite a great looking-woman. He can't help noticing that she's reading some kind of report – and it has the word 'penis' on the cover.

After half an hour spent trying to decipher the complete title he gives up and says: 'Er… cxcusc mc, Miss, but, what exactly are you reading?'

The woman smiles and replies: 'Well, it's a little embarrassing, really. I'm a physiologist and I'm reading a report on the connection between nationality and penis size.'

'Really? That's quite unusual; I wouldn't have thought there was a connection at all.'

'Apparently, there is. According to this survey, the French have the longest penises, while the German penis seems to be the thickest. Englishmen, I'm afraid, are faring rather poorly.'

'How fascinating,' the guy replies. 'But let me introduce myself. My name is Hans and I live in Bordeaux.'

I'M GLAD YOU ASKED ME THAT…

A little boy returns from school with some puzzling questions. He's heard a few things he doesn't understand and resolves to go and ask his mum.

'Mum, what's a pussy?'

The mother, startled, has to do some quick thinking.

She fetches an encyclopaedia and opens it at the page where there is a picture of a cat.

'Here,' she tells her son. 'that's a pussy.'

'I see,' the boy says, although it doesn't seem right. 'And what's a bitch?'

His mum takes a deep breath and shows him a picture of a dog. 'That's a bitch,' she says, proud of having avoided the worst.

The little boy senses something is amiss and decides to get a second opinion. He goes to see his dad in the garage and asks him: 'Dad, what's a pussy?'

The dad is startled by the question, but has a good idea why his son is asking: he's probably heard about it at school. He rummages around the garage for a little while and picks up a dusty cardboard box from a pile of stuff in a forgotten corner. He opens it and admires the photo of a naked lady for a second or two, lost in memories, then picks up a pencil and draws a circle around the woman's vagina.

'This, my son, is a pussy.'

The son is beaming: that's more like it. Emboldened by his dad's broad grin, he asks the second question: 'And what's a bitch?'

The father loses his smile and says: 'Everything outside the circle.'

EVER THE GENTLEMAN

Three men are in a pub discussing sex.

The first one says, 'My wife: when I finish making love to her, it's so good, she's floating five inches above the bed,' says the first one.

The second retorts: 'Well, *my* wife: when I'm done with her, she's floating *10* inches above what's left of the bed.'

The last man says: 'When I'm done shagging my wife, I wipe my dick on the curtains and she hits the fucking roof!'

STICK TO WHAT YOU KNOW

A man is in love with two women and he doesn't know which one to marry. He decides to give them each £100 for a day and see what they do with the money.

One of them puts some of the money into a savings account and buys a lawnmower and some vouchers with what she had left.

The other one buys a couple of CDs, a lamp, some nice coffee and a pack of beers.

So which one will he marry?

The one with the biggest boobs!

DON'T YOU JUST HATE IT WHEN THAT HAPPENS?

A young woman and her lover are busy one summer afternoon but just as the woman turns over to adopt a more provocative position, a bee enters the room. Annoyed at the intrusion, the young man waves it off. The angry bee, disorientated, flies around… and slips into the woman's vagina.

'Oh my God!' she shouts. 'Do something! I have a bee inside me!'

The young man has no idea whatsoever what to do, so he takes her to the nearest GP.

'We were... well, having a bit of fun when this bee entered my girlfriend's vagina,' the man explains, red-faced. 'It's still there and we don't know how to get rid of it.'

'A bee, eh? In the vagina?' The doctor thinks for a minute and then comes up with a solution.

'Tell you what. I'm going to smear some honey on my penis and place it near your girlfriend's vagina. It might entice the bee to come out. What do you say? I need your permission for this, as you can understand.'

'Whatever it takes, doctor: just get it out.'

The good doctor asks the woman to lie on the examination couch and to spread her legs. He takes his trousers down and dips his penis in a little jar of honey.

'It doesn't seem to be working. I fear I might need to penetrate her to show the bee there is a greater prize to be had.'

The woman agrees and the doctor enters her.

'Mmm... I'll have to get in a bit deeper; this bee is a stubborn character.' He enters the woman fully and starts moving in and out. This doesn't seem to be bothering the woman, who after a while seems to forget about the bee. The doctor too becomes more insistent, and starts humping her quite thoroughly.

'Hey, hold on a minute!' the lover objects. 'What do you think you're doing?'

'Change of plan,' pants the doctor. 'I'm going to drown the bastard!'

WORKS EVERY TIME

A guy is about to get married and he confesses to his best mate that he's not sure his future wife is a virgin.

'That's easy to check out,' the friend says with confidence. 'All you need is some blue paint, some red paint and a shovel. When you have that, you paint one of your balls red and the other blue. If she laughs at you and says that they're the funniest pair of balls she's ever seen, whack her with the shovel.'

BETTER LATE THAN NEVER

Two spinsters have been getting old together all their lives, and now they *are* old. One night, Eleanor has had enough. 'I can't stand it any more,' she bursts out. 'I'm not going to die a virgin. I'm going out and I'm not coming back until I've got laid.'

She climbs up to her bedroom, spends an hour getting presentable and comes down again.

'Don't wait for me tonight; I'm out on the town.'

Gladys sighs and resigns herself. She is still feeling a bit shy about sex but does want Eleanor to have some fun in her life if she wants to. She nonetheless waits for her and goes to bed far later than usual. She's drifting off to sleep when she hears the front door open and then slam shut. She just has time to put her dressing-gown on and see Eleanor rush to the bathroom. She follows her and has a peek. Eleanor is sitting on the toilet, her pants around her ankles and looking down at her vagina.

'What are you doing Eleanor? You're OK?'

'Tell you what, Gladys,' Eleanor answers excitedly. 'It was ten inches long when it got in and only five when it got out. When I find the bit that's left, you're going to have the time of your life.'

THANKS FOR SHARING

A man goes to confession: 'Father, I am 80 years old and I just made love to two 20-year-old twins. Twice.'

'I see. And when was the last time you went to confession?'

'Oh, never: I'm Jewish.'

'So why are you telling me this?'

'Well, father, I'm telling everybody!'

HOW SOON THEY FORGET

A man is watching soft porn on TV and is soon aroused, to the point when he asks his wife, who's doing the dishes, to come over and have a smooch.

'Honey bunny, why don't you come and give your darling husband a mucho smoocho?'

His wife agrees with a giggle and walks over to him. On the way, however, she catches her foot in the carpet and falls flat on her face.

'Ohhh... My little honey bunny sweetie pie: you hurt your little nosey-posey-boo? Come here; I'll kiss it better.'

She sits on the sofa next to him he comforts her and soon they are making passionate love. When they are done, the wife rolls off the sofa and heads for the bathroom. On her way, she stumbles on a toy left on the floor by the kids and falls flat on her face again.

Her husband looks at her in disbelief, rolls over and mutters under his breath: 'Clumsy bitch.'

WORTH EVERY PENNY

A man is scheduled for a vasectomy. He goes to hospital for a preliminary appointment, just to have a look around and get a feel of what his operation is going to be like.

He follows a pretty little nurse around the corridors. She stops in front of a door, peeks in and says to the future patient: 'Here, have a look. One of the patients is receiving his post-operative treatment.'

The guy leans over and has a look in the room. Sitting in a bed, a guy is being given a hand job by a ravishing young brunette.

'Er.., interesting,' is all the guy manages to say.

They carry on and come upon a second door, through which little cries of pleasure and muffled sounds can be heard. The nurse opens the door quietly and says: 'Here you go again; another patient receiving post-operative treatment.' The guy has a peek and witnesses a patient wearing a hospital gown being given a blow-job by a young blonde nurse dressed in a Playboy bunny suit.

'Hold on,' he says to the nurse once the door is closed again. 'How come the other guy got a hand job and this one gets oral sex? Is he more gravely ill?'

'Oh no, nothing like that: a vasectomy's a piece of cake, really,' the pert little nurse answers. 'No, you see, the first one was with the NHS and the other with BUPA.'

I'VE GOT HIM FINGERED

A young woman brings her boyfriend home for dinner at her parents' house. Everything's fine, they're all having a great time and dad is showing off by flicking peanuts in the air and catching them in his mouth. Suddenly dad coughs, splutters and starts turning blue.

'He's choking!' his wife exclaims. She rushes to thump him on the back, to no avail. The boyfriend steps forward and pushes the woman away. He grabs the father, puts a finger in each nostril and hits him hard in the back. The peanut is projected out of Dad's mouth and smashes a small glass decanter to pieces. The mother is relieved and the daughter is beaming at her boyfriend, a smile full of unspoken promises on her lips.

Later on that evening, when everyone's gone to bed, the mother snuggles up to her husband and says: 'What a night, eh? I wonder what this boyfriend of hers will do when he's finished university. He could be a doctor.'

'Well,' the father replies, 'I dunno about that, but by the smell of his fingers I reckon he's gonna be our son-in-law at any rate.'

WORKING HER PASSAGE

A young woman is sitting on the promenade wall, facing the beach and the endless sea. She's had an affair with her boss: now she's been sacked and she's lost her boyfriend too. She is disconsolate. A young man approaches and sees her crying her heart out.

'What's the matter?' he asks gently.

She tells him her story. 'I wish I could just board a boat and get the hell out of here: I've had enough of this place.'

'Why don't you?'

'I haven't got the money!' she wails.

The young man thinks it over and then says: 'Listen: I work on a liner and I can smuggle you to America. I'll get you on to the ship in the back of my van and then hide you in my cabin.'

'Really?'

'It'll work, if we're quiet about it, but you might want to do something for me in return.'

The young woman can easily imagine what this 'something' is, but the guy's quite good-looking and she's got nothing to lose, so she agrees. She climbs into the back of the van. They drive for a couple of hours and then the van stops. She hears foreign voices shouting commands and then she feels the unmistakable sway of the sea.

The man opens the back of the van surreptitiously and leads her to a little room. There's just enough space to lie down, which they do before making passionate love.

This goes on for some time. The woman isn't bothered: he gets her food; there's a light at the back so she can read if she wants to and she can use the cabin's toilet and washing facilities – however simple they are. At regular intervals the bloke turns up and they have sex, which is OK with her too.

She can't really say how long this has been going on when the door to her cubicle opens. This time, however, it is not her young man who appears at the door but a man in uniform. She is taken to see the captain.

'So, what have we here? A stowaway?' he asks her in a commanding tone.

'Sir, I was just fed-up with the world, and I met this guy. He promised to take me to America. In return, he screws me.'

'Indeed he does, young lady,' the captain says with a sigh. 'This is the Dover-Calais ferry.'

LEAD US NOT INTO TEMPTATION

Three couples have lived comfortable lives and are quite happy, but they feel there's something missing. They search their souls and decide to go back to church.

'I'd be very happy to welcome you back to the bosom of our church,' the vicar says, 'but you'll have to convince me that you really want to live your lives according to the Lord's rules. You'll have to show me that you are dedicated to being worthy members of our community.'

The three couples agree.

'There is a simple test to perform. I would like you to show me you are strong enough to be Christians again. I would like you to stop having sex for a month.'

The three couples are a bit surprised, but reflect that the change will do them good anyway, so they agree not to have sex for a month. They all go their separate ways, fasting, praying and doing whatever it is that Christian people do instead of having sex, and come back to the vicar a month later.

'So, my children, did you manage to resist temptation and live a life without sin?' the vicar asks the first couple.

'We did,' says the husband.

'Yes: we didn't make love for a whole month!' the wife agrees. Everybody claps and rejoices, for they can now be welcomed into the church.

'What about you two? Was it difficult? Did you conquer the demons of the flesh?'

'Father, we've been married for 40 years. We've found solace in one another's embrace through rain and high tides. It *was* difficult,' the second husband says.

'But we did it,' his wife finishes, holding her man close to her.

The crowd in the church cheers.

'You are the youngest couple of the three,' the vicar says to the last couple. 'I guess it was even more difficult for you, wasn't it?'

'Yes it was,' the wife replies, her eyes downcast.

'She's not to blame,' her husband explains. 'It's just that… Well, we were doing well, I swear, but one day she bent over to reach a tin of baked beans. I just couldn't help myself, I grabbed her and made love to her on the floor there and then. It was too much.'

'Don't blame him either, Father,' the wife cries. 'I'd been dreaming for days that he'd take me. In our minds, we'd already made love.'

The congregation sighs and the vicar nods in understanding.

'You will understand that I can't welcome you into this church in these conditions,' he tells them.

'Yeah, I can understand,' the man says. 'We're not welcome at Safeway any more, either.'

THE FIVE STAGES OF SEX

The first one is called *Perpetual Sex*. This is when you go at it all the time and can't be satisfied. This is usually at the beginning of a relationship.

The second one is called *Kitchen Floor Sex*. This is when you have moved in together and you do it anywhere, especially on the sofa while watching Coronation Street or when you're preparing dinner together.

The third stage is called *Sunday Bedroom Sex*. This is

when you have been together for a while and don't want to be caught doing it by the kids in the next room. It is also called this because Sunday is the only day when neither of you is working or taking the offspring to swimming lessons.

The fourth stage is called *Corridor Sex*. This is when you've been together too long and you pass one another in the corridor and one of you says: 'Fuck you' to the other.

The fifth and final stage of sex is called *Courtroom Sex*, where your wife divorces you and screws you in front of everybody in court.

SWEET DREAMS

A 75-year-old woman goes to her GP. He asks her how she feels: she says she's fine. 'I would like you to do me a favour, though', she tells the doctor. 'I'd like you to put me back on the pill.'

'On the pill? I don't mean to be rude, but… you're 75 years old: you can't get pregnant again, you know,' the doctor replies, quite surprised.

'Oh, I know that,' the little old lady chuckles. 'They make me sleep better.'

The GP is flabbergasted. 'How come the pill makes you sleep better? I've never come across this side effect before.'

'It's quite simple,' the lady explains. 'Every night I put a pill in my granddaughter's orange juice. This way I sleep better.'

NEEDS MUST

Two men go camping for a fortnight. Everything is fine, but, at the end of the first week they've kind of had enough of one another and are bickering more than is acceptable for a holiday. They decide to separate for a couple of days. One will go north while the other goes west. They'll make a loop and meet again in two days.

Two days later, they link up.

'I had a great time,' says the first guy. 'I really think we needed to have some time on our own. I could appreciate the wilderness and the silence.'

'Yes, you're right,' replies the second friend. 'I had a good time too. I had this incredible adventure. I met a woman. She was tied up to some railway tracks that run off in that direction somewhere. I untied her and we made love all night.'

His friend can't believe it. 'What? You go off on your own and you find a woman just like that? Was she pretty?'

'Dunno,' the other guy says. 'Couldn't find her head.'

BUM RAP

First sperm to second sperm: 'No need to hurry; we're not going anywhere.'

Second sperm to first sperm: 'Yeah. We're in deep shit.'

IT'S A WISE CHILD...

Andy is 24. He's loved Amy, the girl next door, since they were together in nursery. He comes home one day and tells his parents that he wants to marry her.

'Well,' the dad says with a side glance to his wife, 'I am afraid it's not possible. You see, I was unfaithful to your mum with Amy's mother. Amy's your half-sister. It was a long time ago,' he finishes lamely.

Andy is devastated. He casts a black look at his dad and storms off. They don't see him for a week.

After a week has passed, he comes back. 'You remember little Rosalyn, who used to live near the butcher's? Well, we're going to get married!'

His mum is over the moon. His dad, though, doesn't look so pleased. 'Well, Andy, I wasn't unfaithful only with Amy's mum: I had a fling with Rosalyn's mother when we were both younger. Rosalyn's your half-sister.'

'I can't believe it!' Andy wails. 'Did you bed the mums of all my childhood friends?' He storms off and locks himself up in his bedroom.

A few minutes pass and there is a knock on his door. His mum silently comes in.

'Come on: you're not going to make a fuss about this, are you?'

'And why not? I can't marry the girls of my dreams because they're my half-sisters!'

'I shouldn't worry about this too much,' she says with a little smile. 'You see, he's not really your father.'

I LOVE MY JOB

A fresh new prostitute is starting today. The older girls have spent the previous evening giving her all sorts of advice and today's her first day. They all look at her as she takes her first client upstairs.

Some time later the client comes down, looking satisfied, quickly followed by the apprentice prostitute.

'So, how was it?' they ask her.

'Well, I asked to be paid in advance, as you told me.'

The other prostitutes nod in agreement.

'Then I told him the prices: £200 for the full game, but he said he couldn't afford that. Then I said it's £100 for a blow-job, but apparently he had only £50. So I told him for that, he could have a hand job.'

The veterans nod again.

'So he gets his pants down and I take him in my hand: then I take him in both hands. Girls, this guy was absolutely huge!'

'So what did you do?'

'I lent him £150.'

MANY A SLIP

A couple are in North Africa. They go to the beach, visit the best restaurants and tour the local markets to find the perfect presents for their friends back home. It is during one of these outings that they come across this Arab merchant and his 'love slippers'.

'Love slippers? What on Earth are these?' the husband asks, holding a pair of ordinary looking shoes.

'Ah, you see, noble sir, this is a pair of love slippers. They are very rare. If you put them on, you'll feel like making love like a camel in heat.'

'Rubbish!' the guy says and puts the slippers back where he found them.

'No, I assure you! These are indeed love slippers that will make you the king of lovers to all the houris you will meet.'

The husband snorts in disbelief but his wife is egging him on.

'Come on,' she says. 'Try them on: maybe you can wear them tonight,' she carries on, with a knowing smile.

Seeing that there is no way out, he puts the shoes on… and suddenly he lets go a mighty groan, puffs up his chest and grabs the merchant. He turns him around and pulls his pants down, ready to have a good go at back-door sex. The merchant squeaks and starts shouting frantically: 'You put them on the wrong feet! You put them on the wrong feet!'

HE'S GOT BOTTLE

A couple are playing golf. The woman isn't that good, and what's supposed to happen when someone who isn't that good plays golf happens: she swings and her ball hits the window of a house. They hear the sound of glass shattering. They decide it would only be proper to go and apologise.

They walk to the house and notice that the ball has smashed the front window. As the door is open, they go in. There is an old man sitting in an armchair waiting for them.

'I assume it was you who smashed the window?'

'Yes, it was; I'm very sorry,' the woman starts.

'I assume, then, that it is your ball which smashed into this bottle of very expensive brandy?' the old man says, pointing to a posh-looking crystal decanter in pieces on the floor.

The woman nods, near to tears.

'Thank you! You see, I am a genie. I've been locked in this bottle for 200 years and you freed me. I will reward you with a wish.'

The man looks at his wife in total puzzlement.

'Er… OK. I wish, I wish… I had a mansion just like yours.'

'It is done,' the genie says with a wave of his hand. 'Now *I* have a favour to ask. I haven't had sex in 200 years. I would really like to make love to a beautiful lady. In reward, I will grant you another wish.'

The husband starts to protest but his wife hushes him: 'Think about it! He's a genie. He could do anything to us. He could kill us or something – or he could make us rich beyond our dreams.'

The husband finally agrees and the genie takes the woman upstairs.

They are having a wonderful time, the woman soon forgetting her previous qualms, when the man giggles.

'Tell me: how old are you both?'

'I'm 42 and my husband is 45,' she pants, nearing her climax.

'A bit old still to believe in genies, wouldn't you say?'

FANTASTIC VOYAGE

First sperm to second sperm: 'Are we there yet?'

Second sperm to first sperm: 'I'm afraid not. We've only just passed the tonsils.'

COME FLY WITH ME

A stunning young woman is about to board a bus. The only problem is that she's wearing one of those very tight miniskirts. It moulds her ass perfectly, but she can hardly move her legs. She tries to bend her knees to negotiate the step to the bus, but she can't.

With a silvery laugh, she reaches behind and unzips her skirt just a tad, to no avail. She still can't raise her leg high enough. She smiles nervously, aware that there are people behind her trying to get on the bus, and unzips her skirt a bit more. It's quite difficult because she's got to reach right behind her back. Anyway, it still doesn't work. She unzips a bit more but it's still not enough.

At this point, the man in the queue behind her picks her up by the hips, lifts her up and deposits her on the step.

The woman is not pleased. She turns around and admonishes the guy: 'Who are you to presume you can do that to me?'

'Well,' the guy replies. 'Seeing that you've been unzipping my fly for the last few minutes, I thought we were friends.'

CONFESSION TIME

This couple have been together for 40 years. Now in their old age together, they're lying in bed after sex. The husband looks at his wife with adoration and says: 'Honey, we've been together a long time. I love you. I'd like to know: have you ever cheated on me? I promise I won't get mad.'

His wife stares at him for a minute, then bursts into tears.

'I have, darling, I have. I'm sorry. I cheated on you three times – but I always had a good reason, believe me.'

'It's OK, babe. Forty years together: I couldn't expect you to be faithful all the time. Tell me: who was the first man? Do I know him?'

'Yes, you do,' the wife replies through her tears. 'Do you remember that we were denied this loan to buy the house?

We wanted to have children and the house wasn't big enough. So I went to McNamara, our bank manager, and was unfaithful to you. That's how we got this loan.'

The man ponders for a while, then says: 'It's OK, honey. I can see you did it for the family. There's nothing to be ashamed of. You were quite courageous and forward-thinking. What about the second time?'

'Do you remember when you had your first heart incident? You needed an operation, quick, but the doctor said there wasn't a bed available for you? Oh, I thought I was going to lose you… I was terrified… so I cheated on you to change the doctor's mind and you got the operation,' she sniffs.

The guy is swelling with pride for his wife. 'You did it for me? What a brave heart you have. And I never knew! This wasn't about cheating; this was about saving my life! And the third time: what happened?'

'Well, do you remember when you *really* wanted to be admitted to that golf club but you were 17 votes short for membership?'

HARD SELL

The company manufacturing Viagra has been contracting an advertising agency to promote its product and find a new slogan. The advertising company came back to them with something suitably catchy: Viagra. Just Do Her.

USING HIS HEAD

A guy sticks his head round the door of the barber's shop and asks: 'How long before I can get a haircut?'

The barber looks around the shop and replies: 'About two hours.'

The guy leaves and doesn't come back. A few days later, the same guy sticks his head round the door and asks: 'How long before I can get a haircut?'

The barber looks around the shop full of customers and says: 'About two hours.'

The guy leaves and doesn't come back.

A week later, the same guy sticks his head in the shop and asks: 'How long before I can get a haircut?'

The barber looks around the shop and replies: 'About an hour and a half.'

The guy leaves.

The barber looks over at a friend in the shop and says, 'Hey, Bill: follow that guy and see where he goes.' In a little while, Bill comes back into the shop laughing hysterically.

'So where did he go when he left here?'

Bill grins and says: 'To your house.'

SO NOW YOU KNOW

What's the definition of 'indecent'?

When it's in long, in hard, and in deep, it's in decent.

ONE FOR THE LADIES

A plane passes through a severe storm. The turbulence is awful and things go from bad to worse when one wing is struck by lightning. One passenger, a young woman, loses it and starts screaming. She stands up in the front of the cabin. 'I'm too young to die!' she wails. 'Well, if I'm going to die, I want my last moments to be memorable! No one has ever made me really feel like a woman! Well, I've had it! I need a man. Now! Is there a real man aboard this plane?'

For a moment there is silence. The blazing wing and the turbulence are forgotten. They all stare, riveted, at the desperate woman in the front of the cabin.

Then a man stands up in the back row.

'I can make you feel like a woman,' he says in a deep, throaty voice.

He's gorgeous: tall, muscular, with square jaws and deep-set brown eyes. Slowly he walks up the aisle, unfastening his shirt one button at a time. No one moves. The woman is breathing heavily in anticipation as the strange man approaches. He removes his shirt. Muscles ripple across his chest as he reaches her. Holding his shirt out to the trembling woman, he whispers: 'Iron this.'

DARWIN WAS RIGHT

Why did God invent lesbians?

So that feminists wouldn't breed.

SHAFTED

A guy of diminutive stature is in a lift to the 24th floor. The lift stops at the second floor and a huge man comes in. He's very impressive, especially to this little guy. He can't keep his eyes off him, having a fantasy of himself looking strong and muscular instead of weedy and weak.

The big guy catches the little man staring at him and says in a booming voice: 'Seven feet tall, 350 pounds, 20-

inch penis, three-pound left testicle, three-pound right testicle, Turner Brown.'

The little guy gasps, recoils into one corner of the lift and promptly faints. After a few seconds he comes to and sees this huge mass of muscles loom above him. He scrambles to his feet and hugs the walls of the cabin.

'What's the matter with you?' the big guy says.

Shyly, the little bloke answers: 'Could... could you repeat what you just said?'

'I just said what I always say to people who meet me for the first time. I know what's going through their minds. I'm seven feet tall, I weigh 350 pounds, I have a 20-inch penis, my left testicle weighs three pounds, my right testicle weighs three pounds and my name is Turner Brown.'

'Oh, I see,' the little guy laughs weakly. 'That's a relief. For a minute there I thought you said, "Turn around."'

TOO LATE, TOO LATE

At a cocktail party, one woman says to another: 'Aren't you wearing your wedding ring on the wrong finger?'

'Yes, I am,' she replies. 'I married the wrong man.'

HOME PHILOSOPHY

Man is incomplete until he is married. Then he's finished.

SPUD U LIKE

An Irishman's in the South of France alone on holiday. He befriends a French guy, Pierre, who goes with a different woman every night. After a while, the Irishman becomes puzzled. Pierre's good-looking, but so is he. Why is he failing to score when Pierre attracts so many girls on the beach?

One day, he's had enough and asks Pierre: 'Tell me; you have a trick, right?'

Pierre laughs and says: 'Yes, my little Irish friend: here!' He tosses him a potato. 'Tuck that into your pants. It drives the women wild.'

'Cheers, mate!' the Irish guy says. He tucks the potato in his pants as instructed and leaves for the beach… where nothing happens. On the contrary, the girls seem to take one look at him and avert their eyes in disgust. Fearing foul play, he goes to see Pierre again.

'It didn't work! You're having one on me there, aren't you?'

'Er…' Pierre replies, 'The potato goes at the front.'

IF ONLY

In a biology class, the teacher has a trick question for his first-year female students: 'Who can name the organ of the human body which, under the appropriate conditions, expands to six times its normal size, and define those conditions?'

Everyone gasps. This is so gross. Eleanor, a stuck-up little brat whose parents have far too much money for her to have sense, exclaims: 'This is not a question to ask us! You'll hear from my parents, I can assure you!'

At this moment, another girl raises her hand and answers: 'The pupil in dim light.'

'Well done,' the teacher congratulates the student with

a chuckle. 'And let me tell you three things, Eleanor. First, you didn't learn your lesson for today. Second, you have a dirty mind and third, you are heading towards a life full of disappointments.'

CURRENT AFFAIR

An elderly couple are having a cup of tea in a café in town. They are celebrating the first time they made love together.

'It was 50 years ago; do you remember? In a field near the canal. You were a pretty hot little number!' the man says with a crooked smile.

'You were quite a horny bastard yourself,' the woman replies. 'The way you took me from behind, on our first time together. I had to hold on to the fence!'

They smile fondly at the memory and then the woman says: 'You know what? Let's go back there and do it again, for old time's sake. Do you think you still can?'

'Wife, this isn't something to ask a man!' he replies with a laugh and off they go.

The waiter, who's witnessed the exchange, decides to follow them. He reckons it would be good fun to watch a couple of pensioners do it and it'll be a hilarious story to tell tonight down the pub.

The three of them – the couple a few step ahead and the waiter following – amble down to the canal. Hand in hand, the husband and wife look around and find the spot where they made love for the first time together, 50 years ago. They face one another, laugh and the man takes his pants off. The little old lady hikes up her skirts, pulls down her panties and grabs the fence.

There followed the most athletic sex the waiter has ever seen. The man goes at it mightily, humping his wife savagely and she responds with powerful hip thrusts. It lasts a good 20 minutes, after which they both fall on the ground, exhausted. The guy is astounded: humbled, even. He's never seen or heard of such a sexual display. He is a bit worried about the couple though, because they haven't been moving for ten minutes. He is about to walk to them and blow his cover, when he sees the man twitch and painstakingly sit up. As his wife does the same, he groans: 'Man, that was a surprise… this fence wasn't electrified 50 years ago.'

KAMI-KHARZI

This plane is crammed with the latest technological gadgets available. It's the pride and joy of the company. It has sockets for laptops, the backs of the seats are moulded to accommodate a TV screen and there's a drink dispenser on every arm rest.

All this is very well and good, but it doesn't do anything for this guy. He wants to pee but, of course, it doesn't matter how advanced a plane is: the gents is *always* full.

'I really need to go,' he says to the flight attendant. 'The male toilets are always engaged. Please, please let me use the ladies'. I promise I won't be long!'

The flight attendant isn't sure.

'OK,' she says after a minute, considering the guy's plight, 'But you'll have to promise me not to touch anything, OK?'

The guy is ready to promise *anything* and is allowed in the female toilets.

Once in there, he notices three buttons. Crazy with relief, he absently presses the first button. A gentle spray of scented water cleans his ass.

'Wow: that felt good,' he thinks. He remembers his promise not to touch anything, but what the hell: he's a grown man, he knows what he is doing, so he presses the second button. A fine duct of talcum powder is puffed on his balls. 'Even better!' he thinks, wondering what the third button does. He presses the last button… and wakes up in hospital. He's lying in bed, his legs strapped in a sling and his groin hurting him terribly.

'Where am I?' he asks a passing nurse.

'You had to press the last button, didn't you?' she asks him. 'They had to land the plane in an emergency for you, you know.'

'All right, I pressed the button. What happened?'

'Well, it was the tampon removal button. Your balls are under your pillow.'

TRUE CONFESSIONS

A nun hails a cab. A taxi stops: she gets in and asks for an address in town. After a few minutes, she notices the driver staring at her in his mirror.

'Are you all right, my son?' she asks him sweetly.

'I'm fine, er… Sister,' he replies. Then, after a minute of silence, he adds: 'If you don't mind me asking, I've always wondered… You lot make vows of celibacy, right?'

'That's true, my son,' the nun replies.

'You never feel the sexual urge? Or if you do, what do you do about it?'

'Oh, we do indeed,' replies the nun with another sweet smile. 'I myself have always wondered what it was like.'

'You have?'

'Well, of course! I am a nun, but that doesn't mean I'm not curious.'

The cab driver is silent for another minute, then blurts out: 'I could show you, maybe.'

It's the nun's turn to be silent for a minute.

'What, here?' she asks finally. 'It's a bit cramped, isn't it? '

'Well, we could try oral sex.'

'Oral sex? I didn't know such a thing existed. Well, maybe I should let you show me.'

The taxi-driver stops the cab in a dark alley and unbuttons his pants. The nun climbs into the front and, after fumbling for a moment, performs the best ever blow-job on him the guy's ever experienced.

'Sister, you're an exceptional woman,' he says to the nun when she's done. 'That was the best oral sex in my life. You're very good at it.'

'I know,' the nun answers now with a deep voice. 'I'm not actually a nun. I'm going to a fancy dress party and my name's Bernard.'

PUCK ME

Two Canadian women are at a bar. One says, 'You know, 80 percent of all men think the best way to end an argument is to make love.'

'Well,' her friend replies,' that'll certainly revolutionise the game of hockey!'

WELL ENDOWED

Two friends are sitting in a pub, staring darkly at a guy sitting at the other end of the bar.

'I don't get it,' says the first guy. 'He's not good-looking, he has absolutely no taste in clothes and he drives a battered old wreck of a car, yet he always manages to go home with the most beautiful women here!'

'Yeah,' replies the other, 'He's not even very funny or anything. All he does is sit there and lick his eyebrows.'

TRY THIS AT HOME

Two guys are in a pub. They have a drink, then another, then yet another, and it goes on like that until closing time.

The first guy moans. 'I'm in trouble now. I know I shouldn't have stayed in the pub that long. Now my wife's going to yell at me when I come back.'

'Mine won't,' the other says smugly.

'Why not? She's not mad at you?'

'Oh, I suppose she is, but when I come back from a late night, I get into bed and I say: 'How about a blow-job?' Strangely enough, I've found out that she's always asleep then.'

WHO'S SCREWING WHO?

Two couples are playing poker one evening when John accidentally drops some cards on the floor. He bends down under the table to pick them up and notices that

Bill's wife Helen isn't wearing any knickers. Quite shocked, John emerges from underneath the table rather red-faced.

The game ends and he goes to the kitchen for a well-earned drink. To his embarrassment, Bill's wife follows him.

'Did you see anything unusual while you were under the table?'

'Er… I guess so…' John answers.

'Well, you can have it all, but it will cost you £500,' Helen purrs. This is just what he's earned at poker for the night, so after the initial shock, John finds himself considering the offer.

'Bill's at work on Friday afternoons. Are you free?' John is. 'What about Friday afternoon at 2pm, then?'

It's a date.

Thursday comes and goes and now it's Friday. His heart beating fast, John drives up to Bill's house. Helen lets him in and pockets the £500. Soon they're shagging like rabbits.

Helen makes sure that everything is as usual for when Bill comes back from work and waits for him to return.

Today though, Bill asks rather abruptly if John's been around. Unable to lie, his wife says yes.

'And did he give you £500?'

Sensing her fate approaching and wondering how he got this information, she says that John did indeed give her £500 this very afternoon.

'Good. He came and borrowed £500 from me this morning and told me he'd come round and give the money back to you this afternoon.'

Chapter 11
Police jokes

GOBBY BOBBY

A rookie is anxious to assert his authority. He is patrolling the streets, eagle-eyed, in the company of an old veteran when they receive a call asking them to disperse a small crowd which is causing trouble near a pub.

They drive there and, sure enough, there is a small crowd on the pavement. His colleague stops the car. The rookie gets out and walks towards the crowd with a very macho gait.

'The fun's over, citizens. Time to go back home now,' he says gruffly.

No one moves.

'I said to go back home now people. We don't want any trouble, do we?' he threatens.

Slowly, reluctantly, they start shuffling off.

Satisfied, he goes back to the car and asks his more experienced colleague who's been waiting for him: 'So, how did I do?'

'Not bad,' he replied with a chuckle. 'Not bad at all, considering that this is a bus stop.'

JUST IN TIME

Police are warning all men who frequent clubs, parties and pubs to be alert and stay cautious when offered a drink by any woman. Many females use a date rape drug called 'Beer' to target unsuspecting men. The drug is generally found in liquid form and is now available almost anywhere. It comes in bottles, cans, from taps and in large 'kegs.' Beer is used by female sexual predators at parties and bars to persuade their male victims to go home and have sex with them. Typically, a woman needs only to persuade a guy to consume a few units of Beer, and then simply ask him home for no-strings-attached sex. Men are rendered helpless against this approach. After several beers, men will often succumb to desires to perform sexual acts on horrific-looking women to whom they would never normally be attracted. After drinking Beer men often awaken with only hazy memories of exactly what happened to them the night before, often with just a vague feeling that something 'bad' occurred. At other times these unfortunate men are swindled out of their life savings in a familiar scam known as 'a relationship.' It has been reported that in extreme cases, the female may even be shrewd enough to entrap the unsuspecting male into a longer-term form of servitude and punishment referred to as 'marriage'.

Apparently, men are much more susceptible to this scam after Beer is administered and sex is offered by the predatory females.

Please forward this warning to every male you know. If you fall victim to this insidious Beer and the predatory women administering it, there are male support groups with venues in every town where you can discuss the details of your shocking encounter in an open and frank manner with similarly affected, like-minded guys. For the support group nearest you, just look up 'Golf Courses' in the Yellow Pages.

STEP OUT OF THE CAR, SIR

Things not to say to a cop when a cop pulls you over:

I can't reach my licence unless you hold my beer.

Sorry, officer: I didn't realise my radar detector wasn't plugged in.

Aren't you the guy from the Village People?

Hey, you must have been doing 125 to keep up with me: good job.

I thought you had to be in relatively good physical shape to be a police officer.

I was going to be a cop, but I decided to finish high school instead.

Bad cop. No doughnut.

You're not going to check the trunk, are you?

Gee, that gut sure doesn't inspire confidence.

Is it true that people become cops because they're too dumb to work at McDonald's?

Do you know why you pulled me over? OK; just so one of us does.

I was trying to keep up with traffic. Yes, I know there's no other car around: that's how far they are ahead of me.

What do you mean, have I been drinking? You're the trained specialist.

Well, when I reached down to pick up my bag of crack, my gun fell off my lap and got lodged between the brake and the gas pedal, forcing me to speed out of control.

Hey, can you give me another one of those full cavity searches?

YEAH, THAT'LL WIN HIM OVER

A cop catches a guy speeding, so he flashes his lights and the guy pulls over. The cop looks him over, sniffs and asks: 'Sir, have you been drinking? Your eyes are bloodshot.'

'So what?' the guy replies. 'Your eyes are glazed; have you been eating doughnuts?'

VICTIMLESS CRIME

Mr Smith receives a phone call from the police station.

'Mr Smith, we've apprehended the person who stole your wife's credit card. We're waiting for you to pick it up.'

'Oh, let him go,' Mr Smith says.

'What? You don't want to press charges?'

'Nah. Oh – and give him back the card, too. He's been spending half as much as my wife this month.'

FIVE-FINGER DISCOUNT

An unlucky shoplifter has been caught with a Rolex. The plain-clothes store detective takes him to see the manager, who gives him a choice: 'You can either buy this watch, or we call the police.'

The shoplifter thinks for a few seconds, then asks: 'I hadn't planned on spending so much… do you have anything less expensive? Like Timex?'

TO SERVE AND PROTECT

In America, Congress is about to pass a bill to strengthen security. They have to decide which department is to receive the bulk of the money and they have three choices: the Los Angeles Police Department, the FBI or the CIA. Understandably, they all compete to prove they're the best. In the end, an exercise is devised to test which is the most effective at apprehending criminals. The test is quite simple: a unit in each department is asked to find a rabbit in a forest.

The CIA go in first. They place animal informants throughout the forest. They question all plant and mineral witnesses. They bug the trees and the brooks, and tag the fish. After three months of extensive investigations, they conclude that rabbits do not exist.

The FBI go in after them. After two weeks with no more leads than the CIA they burn the forest, killing everything in it, including the rabbit, and make no apologies. They issue a statement explaining that the rabbit had been on a list of wanted terrorists for a long time and sell the burnt land to a jail contractor.

The LAPD go in last. They come out two hours later with a badly-beaten bear. The bear is yelling: 'OK! OK! I did it! I'm a rabbit! I'm a rabbit!'

I'LL BE THE DADDY

An escaped convict breaks into a house and the young couple living there end up tied to the bed, helpless.

Whispering in his wife's ear, the husband says: 'Honey, I know this is a lot to ask, but there's a chance that this is the guy they had a picture of on TV. He's a murderer and he's been in jail for years. He might not have had sex for ages. If he attempts anything, we'll have to be brave. It's the only chance we've got to stay alive.'

The wife nods and replies; 'I'm so glad you are taking it this way: I just heard him say you look cute in your satin pyjama bottoms.'

THIN BLUE LINE

The latest police advertising campaign has attracted very few potential recruits. The force needs men, though, so the entrance examination has to be made easier and Sergeant Smith ends up interviewing John, who doesn't look like policeman material at all. Nonetheless, equal opportunity and all that: Sergeant Smith asks the first question:

'Right, back to basics,' he says in a bored tone. 'Numeracy. What's one plus one?'

John replies: '11'.

The sergeant's eyebrows shoot up. It's not the answer he was looking for but, in a way, it's not an incorrect answer either.

'OK. Literacy next. Give me two days in the week that start with the letter T.'

'Today and tomorrow,' John replies proudly.

Sergeant Smith is aghast. Once again, this guy has kind of answered right, while giving an utterly different answer to what was expected. Knowing that policemen are often asked to think outside the box, he reasons that this John person might prove handy after all.

'I see. General knowledge. Who killed John F Kennedy?'

John is silent. After a minute or so, his eyes downcast, he replies: 'I don't know.'

'No big deal,' Sergeant Smith says. 'Come back to me when you do know.'

'Sure thing. I'll work on it,' replies John. He nods smartly to the sergeant and leaves.

'So, how did the interview go?' his wife asks.

'Pretty good,' John says. 'Only one day at the office and I'm already on a murder case.'

STICK 'EM UP

Bob and Joe are in a bank chatting about this and that when suddenly the door is banged open and armed robbers burst in.

'Nobody move!' one of them barks, while his accomplices rush to the counters, smash the glass and begin transferring handfuls of cash into large plastic bags. Another robber is passing among the hostages, roughly grabbing handbags, watches and jewellery.

Tom is paralysed by fear as the robbers approach him and nearly yells in surprise when he feels something being forced into his hands.

'What's that?' he whispers to Bob from the corner of his mouth, not daring to move his hands to see what Bob has put in there.

'The £50 I owe you,' Joe whispers back.

SEND ME THE BILL

A prisoner receives a letter from his wife. She writes to him about this and that and concludes with a gardening question: 'I remember how you loved to work in the garden, so here's a question for you: I bought some lettuce plants I'd like to plant in the back garden. When is a good time?'

The prisoner doesn't answer straight away, because he knows that all the mail is read by the staff before being given to the prisoner. So he thinks about it for a couple of days, then sends the following message to his wife: 'Honey, you can't plant them in the back garden! Please, don't touch the back garden! I left something there which I want to pick up when I get out of this place.'

A week later, he receives another letter from his wife which concludes: 'By the way, I didn't touch the back garden, as you told me. Unfortunately, a bunch of policemen turned up the other day and dug it all up.'

To which the prisoner writes back: '*Now* is the right time to plant the lettuce.'

CAUGHT ON CAMERA

A guy is just keeping up with the traffic, not realising that by doing so he's breaking the speed limit. What's supposed to happen happens and he gets caught by a mobile camera.

When the police pull him over, he's got his defence ready.

'OK, I know I was speeding, but there were plenty of cars driving just as fast as I did, so why didn't you arrest them?'

'Ever been fishing?' the policeman asked him urbanely.

'Yeah, a couple of times: why?'

'Did you ever catch them all?'

A LOT OF BOTTLE

Tom and Harry are having a great time in the car. The radio's blaring, they're going to a party and the night is young. They're also taking swigs from a four-pack of bottled lager at regular intervals. They're enjoying themselves so much, in fact, that they don't see the speed camera and they get flashed. In the distance, they now see the tell-tale blue lights.

'Damn!' Tom swears. 'Tell you what. Rip off the labels from the bottles, stick them on our foreheads and let me do the talking.'

Harry, quite inebriated, does as he is told. He sticks a label of 1664 on his forehead and one on Tom's and hides the evidence under the seat.

'Good evening, gentlemen,' says the policeman. 'You've been caught driving at 65 and this is a 50 zone.'

'I'm sorry, officer,' Tom replies contritely. 'We're on our way to a party and we're a bit late. I guess I wasn't paying attention.'

The policeman looks at him and says in a suspicious tone: 'Have you been drink-driving?'

Tom points at the label on his forehead and says: 'No, officer. We've quit. We're on the patch.'

NEARLY DEPARTED

A murderer, sitting in the electric chair, is about to be executed.

'Have you any last requests?' asks the chaplain.

'Yes,' replies the murderer. 'Will you hold my hand?'

THAT OLD EXCUSE

Late one Friday night a policeman spots a man driving very erratically through the streets of London. He pulls the man over and asks him if he's been drinking.

'Well, of course I've been drinking,' the man says in a somewhat slurry speech. "It's Friday, and I always drink on Friday. You know what? There's not a decent pub to go to on a Friday night in Dalston. That's why I've got to drive all the way here. Me and me mate had a few beers, as usual: then we switched to whisky. They have a 'buy three, get the fourth one free' offer. I mean, I wasn't gonna let that pass, right? I get paid on Friday night: that doesn't mean I can't be careful about my money, eh? Then I met a couple of mates from work and we had a few more rounds for the road and here I am.'

The policeman sighs and says to the guy: 'I'm sorry, sir; you'll have to take a breathalyser test.'

'What? You don't believe me?' the driver asks indignantly.

ASK A PROFESSIONAL

'Good morning, officer,' a guy says to the policeman behind the desk at the station. 'It's about this guy who broke into my house last night.'

'Yes: how can I help you?'

'Well, I was wondering if I could have a chat with him.'

'I'm sorry, sir, we can't allow that,' the policeman replies. 'You'll get plenty of chances to state your case during the court hearing.'

'Oh, you don't understand,' the guy insists. 'I don't want to insult him or anything: quite the contrary. You see, he managed to get into our house last night without waking up the wife. I've been trying to do exactly that for the past ten years, so I'd like to know how *he* did it.'

LOVELY JUGGLY

A police patrol stops a car at random in a big city. They inspect the car and, to their surprise, find an impressive collection of knives in the boot.

'What are you doing with all these knives?' the officer asks, while the other cop takes his truncheon out of his holster.

'You don't understand,' the driver says. 'I'm an artist, a juggler. I work in a circus. These are my stage knives.'

'Pull the other one.'

'Seriously, officer: let me give you a demonstration.' The officer is inclined to refuse the request but, then again, he's got back-up, so he hands a couple of knives to the guy.

The driver picks them up and shows the policemen that the knives aren't sharp, and then he starts juggling. When it is quite evident that he's not going to harm anyone, the officer lets him juggle with a couple more.

Just at this moment, another car passes by. The driver looks at his wife and says in awed tones: 'Oh, my God!

They're really getting tough with alcohol testing now! Look at what they're asking people to do!'

WHY DIDN'T YOU SAY SO?

The usher of a cinema notices a guy sprawled across three seats in the front row. The cinema isn't full, but this is no reason why this guy should feel entitled to act this way, so the usher goes to him and whispers: 'Sir, could you please sit properly?'

There is no answer. The guy refuses to budge. Irritated, the usher repeats his sentence, to no avail. He decides to fetch the manager.

The manager arrives a few minutes later and orders the guy to sit up properly. There's no answer and the guy refuses to move. 'I'm warning you, sir. If you don't behave in a civil manner, I'll have to call the police.'

All he gets for his pains is a wall of silence, so he decides to carry out his threat and he calls the police.

A policeman turns up and walks to the spot where this guy is sprawled across three seats in a most anti-social manner.

'OK, sir, please be reasonable and sit up properly. You're disrupting the film.'

As there's no answer, he sighs and opens his notebook with exaggerated drama.

'Don't force me to do this, sir,' he warns. 'If you don't behave properly I'll have to take you to the station.' As the guy remains silent, the policeman shrugs and takes the top off his ballpoint pen.

'All right, then. What's your name?' No answer. 'Stubborn to the last, I see,' the policeman chides. 'OK, maybe you don't understand me. Maybe you're not a British citizen.' Slowly and distinctly, he asks: 'Where do you come from?'

The shape on the seat feebly lifts his head and croaks: 'The balcony…'

POPEMOBILE

The Pope is in Great Britain. He's trying to travel incognito and relax a bit in his hired limousine. He watches the British countryside pass by; he sees in the distance the slender spires of country churches, and it makes him feel good. After a couple of hours of that, though, he's getting bored. He taps the driver the shoulder of and says: 'My son, would you indulge an old man in a bit of fun? I've always wanted to drive a big car. Could we swap?'

The driver, not wanting to argue with the pontiff, stops the car and sits at the back.

The Pope is quite happy at the wheel of this huge limousine which he's driving over the limit – not too much, but just enough to be spotted by a patrol car.

The policeman has a look at him and blanches.

'Sergeant,' he says to his superior in the car. 'I don't know if we wouldn't be better off forgetting about this incident.'

'Why? What's the problem?'

'Well, it looks like we've got a pretty important guy in this car.'

'Who is it?'

'I don't know, Sarge: the windows are tinted, but I strongly recommend we get out of here quick.'

'Come off it!' the sergeant scoffs. 'No one's above the law, not even the Prime Minister.'

As the policeman doesn't reply, the sergeant becomes uncertain.

'It's not the Prime Minister, is it?'

'I don't know, Sarge, but this guy's got the Pope as his chauffeur…'

THAT'S GOTTA HURT

A man has just parked his car. He opens up the door to get out and another car speeding by rips the door clean off.

'What?' the guy wails. 'Look at that! My BMW! It's wrecked!'

A passer-by who has witnessed the scene runs to him and says: 'Forget about the door! This car's taken your arm as well; we need to take you to hospital as fast as we can.'

The guy looks down at his left arm in disbelief. It's gone.

'Oh, no!' he wails. 'My Rolex!'

'ELLO, 'ELLO, 'ELLO

Headline: A hole has appeared in one of the walls of the ladies' changing rooms at the sports club. Police are looking into it.

SIMPLE IF YOU KNOW HOW

A young police officer stops a guy who's been speeding. He asks him to get out and the guy complies.

'All right,' the officer says. 'May I see your licence, please?'

'I don't have it any more,' the driver replies. 'You lot took it away last month when I was caught drink-driving.'

'Oh, that's lovely,' the cop says with heavy sarcasm. 'Drink-driving and now speeding with no licence. You have the papers for this car?'

'Dunno. They might be there somewhere: I didn't check when I stole it, I didn't see it in the glove box when I put my gun in there, though.'

'You have a gun in the glove box?' the cop asks nervously.

'I guess I could have left it with the dead guy in the boot, but you never know when this kind of thing might come in handy.'

'There's a corpse in the boot?' the policeman backs up, takes his gun out and feels for his radio through the open window. He's keeping the driver under the barrel of the gun all the time it takes a couple more patrol cars to turn up.

His colleagues take him to the side and the sergeant interrogates the driver.

'I'll need your licence number, if you can remember it.'

Wordlessly, the guy hands out his driving licence. He follows this by the car's papers.

'Everything seems to be in order,' the sergeant says, squinting at the licence and ownership papers. He casts a glance at the policeman who's made the call and is now talking, wild-eyed, to the other policemen a few yards away.

'Let me see this gun of yours now. Easy and slow, if you please.'

'What gun?' the driver asks innocently.

'The officer who arrested you said you had a gun in the glove compartment.'

'There's no gun in there: see for yourself.'

The sergeant opens the car door and has a look in the glove compartment. He finds nothing. He quickly walks to the back of the car and opens the boot.

'Er... why exactly are you looking in the boot, sir?' the guy asks.

'Well, I'll be damned. He called us saying that there was this guy with no licence, no papers for the car, who had a gun and had used it to kill a man he kept hidden in the boot,' the sergeant says, baffled.

'Oh. I see,' replies the driver. 'He's a rookie, is he?'

'Yes.'

'And I bet he said I was speeding too, right?'

THE QUIET LIFE

A policeman stops a tractor on a lane in some Shropshire backwater. He says to the old farmer: 'Sir, do you realise your wife fell out of the cab several miles back?'

'Thank God: I thought I'd gone deaf!' the farmer replies.

THERE'S NO ANSWER TO THAT

A little boy is at the post office with his mum one day. They are at the counter to pay for some stationery when a police officer comes in. He walks to the counter and asks the sales assistant if he can borrow some Sellotape. The clerk hands the sticky tape over and the policeman proceeds to put the picture of a wanted criminal on the wall.

The little boy approaches him and asks: 'This is a photo of somebody you're looking for?'

'It is, son. The detectives want him very badly.'

'If you want him so badly, why didn't you keep him when you took his picture?' he asks the policeman in a puzzled tone.

MUCH BETTER, THANKS

A farmer who's been involved in a terrible road accident with a large lorry ends up in court fighting for a big compensation claim.

The insurance company refuses to give him any money on the grounds that there is no substantial evidence that the farmer has sustained any injury at all.

'You claim that you suffered injuries from this accident?' the judge asks.

'That's right,' the farmer replies.

'I have here a statement, signed by you at the time of the accident,' the judge carries on, picking up a sheet of paper from his desk. 'On here, it clearly states that you told the officer in charge that you were fine.'

'I did, your honour,' the farmer stammers, 'but there's more to it than that.'

'Yes, I know: there always is,' the judge sighs. 'All right: tell me your story and tell me why you're going back on your statement.'

'Well,' the farmer begins. 'I was going to town to sell my horse when this lorry crashed into me, your honour. I didn't really see what happened. All I know is that I must have passed out for a minute or so. There was blood everywhere and my dog had been thrown out of the cab through the windshield. I could see him lying on the tarmac in a pool of blood. His tail was still moving though, so I knew he was still alive. I managed to get out and went to my horse. He was still alive too, barely. I didn't know if he would make it.'

The farmer paused, stressed at the recollection and then carried on: 'Then this cop turned up. He went to the horse. I suppose he thought, like me, that he wouldn't make it, so he got his gun out and shot him dead. Then he went to my dog and shot him too. Then he came to me and asked me how I was feeling. Man, what the hell was I supposed to say?!'

I'LL LET YOU OFF, PROF

It's 2am: the police stop a man in the street and ask for an ID.

'So, what are you doing in the streets at such an hour?' one of the policemen asks while his colleague reads the guy's ID.

'I'm back from giving a lecture,' he replies. 'I'm a lecturer.'

'Ha! Pull the other one. You don't look like a lecturer to me!

His colleague taps him on the shoulder and whispers that his ID says that he is, indeed, a lecturer.

'So what? Who were you giving a lecture to at this time of night anyway?' the policeman asks triumphantly.

'My wife.'

A FATE WORSE THAN DEATH

Two men are scheduled to die in the electric chair on the same day. The chaplain and the director of the prison will assist the proceedings. Before they give the go-ahead for the execution however, they have to perform one last rite: granting the last request of the condemned.

The chaplain approaches the first prisoner and asks him: 'My son, do you have a last request?'

'Yeah, I do,' he replies. 'I'm very fond of music. I'd like to hear a song one last time: the song that was playing on the jukebox when I met my wife. Could you play 'Candle in the Wind' by Elton John for me one last time?'

The chaplain glances sideways at the director of the prison, who nods his agreement.

'Very well,' the father says. 'You will hear this song once more before the execution. What about you, my son?' he asks the other guy. 'Do you have a last request?'

'Yeah,' the prisoner says with a grimace. 'Could you do me first?'

HARD LESSON

'I did stop, officer, honest,' a driver explains for the fourth time to the officer who's just pulled him over for going through a Stop sign.

'You didn't stop, sir,' the policeman explains to him for the fourth time. 'I was driving right behind you. You did slow down, but you didn't stop.'

'Slowing down or stopping: what's the difference?'

At the end of his tether, the policeman grabs his truncheon and proceeds to beat the shit out of the obtuse driver.

'Now,' he asks. 'Would you like me to stop or just slow down a little?'

WITH FRIENDS LIKE THESE ...

A car is stopped by police near Dover. The driver rolls down the window and asks in a friendly tone: 'What's the problem, officer? I wasn't speeding, was I?'

'No, you weren't speeding. In fact, I've been following you for some time and I'd like to congratulate you on your driving. You've been indicating all the time, you've been respecting the speed limits all through town... your driving is exemplary. You know, people always think of us as here to make drivers' lives miserable and give tickets. What very few people know is that we can also reward good drivers, too. This is why I stopped you. I'd like to reward you with a £500 cheque to encourage you to carry on driving the way you do.'

'This is grand,' the guy smiles. 'Now I can get my licence.'

'I told you we shouldn't have stolen this car,' says his mate on the passenger seat.

'Don't pay any attention to him,' the woman at the back says with a little nervous laugh. 'He's always trying to be funny when he's on crack.'

'Why are we stopping?' comes a voice from inside the boot. 'Have we come through the Channel Tunnel yet?'

GO ON, LIVE A LITTLE

A sign on the side of the road warns that there is a bridge ahead and that the maximum headroom is 5.80 metres.

'What do we do?' one of the drivers of a lorry asks his colleague. "We have a clearance of 6.2 metres.

The guy thinks for a few seconds, looks left and right and then says: 'There's no cops. We'll give it a go.'

WISE WORDS

In God we trust. Everybody else is suspect.

OUCH!

A drunk man is walking down the street, his hands to his bloody nose. A cop can't help noticing he seems to have taken a beating.

'Can you describe the person who did this to you, sir?' he asks.

'That's exactly what I was doing when this guy hit me, officer,' he replies.

TOO QUICK FOR HER

A middle-aged woman, who's never been what you can call a beauty, is stopped for speeding.

'I'm fed-up!' she cries to the policeman. 'I'm always the one being picked on. Why is it you guys always want to give me a ticket? Is it my face?'

'No, madam,' the officer replies. 'It's your foot.'

YOU WAIT FOR AGES ...

A young woman, not overly bright, is stranded in London. It's the first time she's been there and she's thoroughly lost. She looks around and, relieved, sees a policeman. She walks up to him and says: 'Good morning, officer. I'm a bit lost.'

'I know the feeling,' the policeman says, with an encouraging smile. 'London's quite a big place. Where is it you want to go?'

'I'd like to go to Oxford Circus.'

'It's not too complicated from here. Just walk down this road, turn left and get the Number 73 bus. It stops at Centre Point, right at the beginning of Oxford Street.'

The young woman thanks him effusively and walks down to catch the bus. As for the policeman, he carries on his tour of duty for a couple of hours. You can understand how surprised he is when he meets the young lady again. She's still waiting for the bus.

'Oh, don't worry about me, officer,' the young lady says with a fluttering of eyelashes. 'Number 68 just passed. It shouldn't take long now.'

A SIDEWAYS LOOK

A policeman was interrogating three blondes who were training to become detectives. To test their skills in recognising a suspect, he shows the first blonde a picture for five seconds and then hides it.

'This is your suspect, how would you recognise him?'

The first blonde answers, 'That's easy: we'll catch him fast because he only has one eye!'

The policeman says, 'Well... uh... that's because the picture shows his profile.'

Slightly flustered by this ridiculous response, he flashes the picture for five seconds at the second blonde and asks her, 'This is your suspect; how would you recognise him?'

The second blonde giggles, flicks her hair and says, 'That shouldn't be too difficult: he only has one ear!'

The policeman angrily responds, 'What's the matter with you two? Of course only one eye and one ear are showing – because it's a picture of his profile! Is that the best answer you can come up with?'

Extremely frustrated at this point, he shows the picture to the third blonde and in a very testy voice asks, 'This is your suspect; how would you recognise him?'

He quickly adds '...Think hard before giving me a stupid answer.'

The blonde looks at the picture intently for a moment and says, 'The suspect wears contact lenses.'

The policeman is surprised and speechless because he really doesn't know himself whether the suspect wears contacts or not. 'Well, that's an interesting answer...wait here for a few minutes while I check his file and I'll get back to you on that.'

He leaves the room and goes to his office, checks the suspect's file in his computer and comes back with a beaming smile on his face. 'Wow! I can't believe it... you're right! The suspect does in fact wear contact lenses. Good work! How were you able to make such an astute observation?'

'That's easy,' the blonde replied. 'He can't wear glasses because he only has one eye and one ear.'

YOU'RE GOING DOWN

A man has been charged with fraud and is now facing the judge. His lawyer, a thoroughly arrogant man, makes his way over to the judge and waves a chequebook.

'He's guilty. I know this; you know this; so let's make it short and I'll write the bail cheque.'

The judge looks him up and down and replies: 'You'll have ample time to present your case later on. For now, let's follow the correct procedure.'

'A man of the financial stature of my client doesn't have time for procedure. Just give me the amount and I'll write the cheque.'

'Very well,' the judge replies, a steely glint in his eyes. 'Please write me out a cheque for six months' imprisonment.'

THE POWER OF THE LORD

A very religious lady comes back from church one evening and catches a burglar in her house. Unfazed and confident in the power of the Bible, she shouts: 'Stop! Acts 2:38!'

The burglar stops dead in his tracks, freezes and drops whatever he had managed to grab. The old lady strides to the telephone and calls the police, who arrive promptly.

'I don't understand,' the policeman says to the old lady, as he's clicking the pair of handcuffs shut on the intruder's wrists. 'What did you tell him?'

'Acts 2:38. Repent and be baptised, every one of you, in the name of Jesus Christ so that your sins may be forgiven,' she explains piously.

'What? I thought she had an axe and two .38s!' exclaims the distraught burglar.

IN OTHER WORDS

Two prostitutes are cruising in search of potential clients. They have come up with a shrewd plan: they have a sticker on the back of the car that reads 'Prostitutes. £100.'

They get stopped by the police. The policeman tells them they are not allowed to advertise for their line of work. As they are waiting by the side of the road, a car passes by with a sticker on the bumper saying: 'Jesus is your saviour. Visit your local church.'

'How come they can advertise and not us?' one of the prostitutes asks.

'This isn't the same thing,' the officer replies patiently. 'This pertains to religious beliefs and is legal.'

The prostitutes get a warning and have to rip the sticker off their car bumper.

Back on the road they remain silent for a while, thinking about what has happened. Suddenly, the one driving shouts: 'I know!' and stops at a roadside service area. She goes to the shop and comes back with a sheet of paper, a pen and some sticky tape. A short time later the car is back on the road proudly wearing a bumper sticker that reads: 'Two angels seeking Peter. £100.'

GREAT BIG ARSE

This guy is driving an expensive car far too fast on the motorway. A police patrol catches him and pulls him over.

'Quite a car you've got there,' the policeman says. 'What is it you do?'

'Me? I'm a rectum-stretcher.'

'A rectum-stretcher?'

'Yeah. It's for people with bowel problems. I insert a finger, then two and I work at it until I open the rectum 10cm wide.'

'Wow! What do you do with a guy with a 10cm wide rectum?'

'Well, you just put him in a car waiting by the side of the road.'

GUILTY AS SIN

A cop sees a car weaving all over the road and pulls it over. He walks up to the car and sees a nice-looking woman behind the wheel. Her breath smells strongly of alcohol.

'I'm going to give you a breathalyser test to determine if you're under the influence of alcohol,' he tells her.

She blows into the tube and watches the cop walk back to the police car. After a couple of minutes he returns and says, 'It looks like you've had a couple of stiff ones.'

'You mean it shows that, too?' she exclaims, horrified.

STIFF SENTENCE

Two burglars have broken into a pharmacy and managed to steal a large quantity of the drug Viagra. The local police are now on the look out for two hardened criminals.

GETTING OFF LIGHTLY

'So tell me, what happened?' an officer asks a young lady who's just sent her husband to A&E with a broken arm.

'He talked to me,' the wife replies.

'Is that it? Do you happen to have a short temper?'

'No, not at all. I'm very even-tempered.'

'So why did you beat him up? Come on: you and your husband were waking up, he speaks to you and you break his arm. What did he say to you?'

'He said: 'Good morning, Lucy"

'Is that all? And you're telling me you don't have a temper?'

'My name's Joanne,' the wife replies between clenched teeth.

LOSING CONTROL

A woman with a car full of little future Premiership footballers goes through a stop sign and almost rams into a police car.

The officer gets out of his car and screams: 'Lady, don't you know when to stop?'

Shame-faced, the lady replied: 'Honest, officer, these kids aren't all mine'.

TOO FAST TO LIVE, TOO YOUNG TO DIE

An old woman is driving down to the shops. On her way, she goes through a red light and is caught by a passing police car.

The cop pulls the car over and leans through the window.

'Madam, where are you going?'

The old woman turns round to her husband, who yells: 'He wants to know where you're going!'

'Oh,' she replies with a little-old-lady smile. 'I'm trying to find a car park. I don't really know my way around here.'

The policeman realises that this old lady hasn't gone through the lights because of recklessness but was confused by the traffic, and decides to let it drop. Wanting to show that cops can be nice people, however, he asks the lady: 'You're not from around here? Where are you from?'

The old lady turns to her husband again. The husband sighs and yells: 'He wants to know where you come from.'

'Oh, Dorset; I was born in Dorset,' she tells the officer with another of her sweet smiles.

'Dorset! Had one of my worst screws in Dorset,' the policeman mutters, *sotto voce*.

'What did he say?' the old lady driver asks her husband.

'He said he think he knows you!' the husband yells back.

Chapter 12

Silly sayings and fascinating facts

SILLY SAYINGS

Man who marry woman with no tits bound to feel low down.

Virginity like bubble: one prick, all gone.

Man who run in front of car get tired.

Man who run behind car get exhausted.

Man with hand in pocket feel cocky all day.

Foolish man give wife grand piano; wise man give wife upright organ.

Man who walk through airport turnstile sideways going to Bangkok.

Man who eat many prunes get good run for money.

Panties not best thing on earth. But next to best thing on earth.

Wife who put husband in doghouse soon find him in cat-house.

Man who fight with wife all day get no piece at night.

It take many nails to build crib, but one screw to fill it.

Man who drive like hell bound to get there.

Man who stand on toilet is high on pot.

Man who fish in other man's well often catch crabs.

If you go to bed with an itchy bum, don't be surprised in the morning to have a smelly finger.

Two wrongs are only the beginning.

A clear conscience is usually the sign of a bad memory.

When all else fails, read the directions.

Happiness can't buy money.

If at first you don't succeed, destroy all evidence you ever tried.

The meek shall inherit the Earth after we're done with it.

A coward is a hero with a wife, kids and a mortgage.

If you ever need a dead battery, look for the torchlight.

Extremists should be shot.

A man is like a snoring radiator.

True friends always stab you in the front.

I'll have to think twice about it before I give it a second thought.

Help stamp out, eliminate and abolish redundancy!

A penny saved is not much

A woman with small tits is like a pair of jeans without pockets: one doesn't know where to put one's hands.

Better late than pregnant.

Beer was invented so that even ugly people can have sex.

If your attack is going really well, it's an ambush.

The problem with living alone is that it's always your turn to do the washing-up.

A day without sunshine is like... night.

Memory is the asshole's intelligence.

Why contradict a woman? All you have to do is wait for her to change her mind.

The best things in life are either immoral, illegal or make you put on weight.

Every year there are more and more assholes, but this year it feels like the assholes of next year are already here.

Tell someone that there are 300 million stars in the universe and they will believe you. Tell them that the paint isn't dry yet and they'll have to touch it to be sure.

It's not an optical illusion; it just looks like one.

What if there were no hypothetical situations?

If you must choose between two evils, pick the one you've never tried before.

Honesty is the best policy, but insanity is a better defence.

Gravity is a myth: the Earth sucks.

Never be nasty to a woman. Nature takes care of that as time passes.

A committee is a group of people who keep minutes and waste hours.

Forgive your enemies, but remember their names.

Stupidity got us into this mess. It will probably get us out too.

After sex, 10 per cent of men turn on their left side, 10 per cent of women turn on their right side and the rest go back home.

One must always finish what one has sta

A man who gets married once deserves a crown for his patience. A man who gets married twice deserves a straightjacket.

Eternity is very long, especially near the end.

When on the ladder of success, don't let boys look up your dress.

Artificial intelligence will never beat natural stupidity.

Experience is a wonderful thing. It enables you to recognise a mistake when you make it again.

If Jesus Christ had been impaled, there would never have been such a thing as Christianity.

Women should put pictures of missing husbands on beer cans.

The only substitute for good manners is fast reflexes.

All those who believe in psychokinesis raise my hand.

Ass-kicking is the electroshock of the poor.

I'll drink milk when cows eat hops.

If money grew on trees, women would marry monkeys.

Love is grand; divorce is a hundred grand.

The real art of conversation is not only to say the right thing at the right time, but also to leave unsaid the wrong thing at the tempting moment.

Great things come to those who wait, but generally they are useless things left by the people who were there before you.

Beauty is in the eye of the beer holder.

War doesn't determine who's right, just who's left.

If it ain't broke, wait a couple of years.

FASCINATING FACTS

If you yelled for eight years, seven months and six days, you would have produced enough sound energy to heat one cup of coffee.

If you fart consistently for six years and nine months, enough gas is produced to create the energy of an atomic bomb.

The human heart creates enough pressure while pumping to squirt blood 30 feet.

Banging your head against a wall uses 150 calories an hour.

Humans and dolphins are the only species that have sex for pleasure.

People fear spiders more than they do death.

The strongest muscle in the body is the tongue.

You can't sneeze with your eyes open.

You can't kill yourself by holding your breath.

Americans, on average, eat 18 acres of pizza every day.

Every time you lick a stamp, you're consuming one-tenth of a calorie.

You are more likely to be killed by a champagne cork than by a poisonous spider.

Right-handed people live, on average, nine years longer than left-handed people do.

A pig's orgasm lasts for 30 minutes.

A crocodile cannot stick its tongue out.

The ant can lift 50 times its own weight, can pull 30 times its own weight and always falls over on its right side when intoxicated.

Polar bears are left-handed.

The catfish has more than 27,000 taste buds, more than any other animal.

The flea can jump 350 times its own length (equivalent to a human jumping the length of a football field).

A cockroach will live nine days without its head. The only reason it doesn't live longer is that it's unable to eat.

The male praying mantis cannot copulate while its head is attached to its body: therefore the female initiates sex by ripping the male's head off.

Some lions mate more than 50 times a day.

Butterflies taste with their feet.

Elephants are the only mammals that can't jump.

A cat's urine glows under a black light.

An ostrich's eye is bigger than its brain.

Starfish haven't got brains.

ORGASM TYPES

Sex in a boat: Oargasms

Sex with a computer programmer: Dorkgasms

Sex in the hallway: Doorgasms

Sex with a dermatologist: Poregasms

Sex with a bullfighter: Toreadorgasms

Sex with a medieval poet: Troubadorgasms

Sex in Asia: Singaporegasms

Sex with someone not paying attention: Ignorgasms

Sex with an Icelandic singer: Bjorkgasms

Sex during hay fever season: Sporegasms

Sex on the kitchen linoleum: Floorgasms

Sex in Safeway: Storegasms

Sex with a prostitute: Whoregasms

Sex with a storyteller: Loregasms

Sex with a tax accountant: Boregasms

Sex somewhere else in Asia: Easttimorgasms

Sex while sleeping: Snoregasms

Sex in the Hundred Acre Wood: Eeyoregasms

Sex when broke: Poorgasms

Sex with a lion: Roargasms

Sex for six hours: Soregasms

Sex with masked avenger: Zorogasms

Sex on the beach: Shoregasms

Sex in the wild: Outdoorgasms

Sex with a meat-eater: Carnivoregasms

Sex with a possessive partner: Yourgasms

Sex with a competitive partner: Scoregasms

Sex with socks on: Odorgasms

Sex in a train: Allaboardgasms

Sex with Cortez: Conquistadorgasms

Sex with a cookie: Oreogasms

Sex while flying a glider: Soargasms

Sex with a religious person: Pastorgasm

Sex with a dog: Labradorgasms

Sex during an earthquake: Tremorgasms

Sex on a farm: Tractorgasms

Sex while drunk: Liquorgasms

Sex with Frankenstein's assistant: Igorgasms

Sex with three of your friends: Fourgasms

Sex with a Norse god: Thorgasms

Sex when resistance is futile: Borggasms

Sex without a climax: Nogasms

LEARNING FROM NATURE

It is the early bird that gets the worm, but the second mouse gets the cheese.

HAPPINESS CAN BE YOURS

This is a good luck scheme letter. Do not bin it or delete it. Send a copy of this letter to five of your friends, then bundle up your wife or girlfriend in a big box and send them to the man whose name appears at the top of this list. When this is done, add your name to the bottom of the list.

If all the friends you have sent this letter to send it back to five of their friends in turn, it could take you as little as a week to receive 16,255 women.

The laws of probability ensure that, amongst these 16,255 women, five per cent will be nymphomaniacs, 20 per cent will be under 30, 31 per cent will not mind giving oral sex, 42 per cent will have had breast implant surgery, 65 per cent will enjoy sex in the bathroom and 90 per cent will be better looking than the woman you've sent.

Think about it: one of them is bound to be better than the one you already have.

At the time of writing this, a friend of mine had already received 184 women, 26 of whom were worth keeping!

DO NOT BREAK THIS CHAIN! One man broke the chain and got his own wife back.

USELESS TRIVIA

If you punch a man in the nose and kick him in the balls at the same time, he can't tell you where it hurts the most.

It takes 1,458,732 times longer to sharpen a knife on a block of butter than it does on a whetstone.

The elephant is the only mammal which can masturbate while keeping its hands free.

The end of the world happened on January 3, 2001, but nobody noticed.

Atheist dogs don't believe in Man.

There is only one place where a grain of sand is more annoying than in between the teeth: in a condom.

A blind man runs just as fast as a deaf man when they smell fire.

Male cats can see in the dark. That's of no use to them, as female cats see in the dark too.

People who were born blind can easily know, just by touching them, whether a dog is black or if it bites.

In the year 2050, three men out of four will be Chinese. The fourth one will be Japanese.

Laughing gas is useless on people with no sense of humour.

When you press on a wart, it may happen that the substance coming out tastes like vanilla custard, but this is an extremely rare occasion.

If you paint a man one-third red, one-third blue and one-third yellow and then make him spin very fast, you'll get the Invisible Man.

Scientists have discovered, thanks to very powerful telescopes, that Venus shows us a planet-sized bum. They are divided as to what Venus' hidden side might show.

A child with an average IQ will suss out the mechanism of a hand grenade in 72 seconds.

When kamikaze fighters flew to their deaths, they closed their eyes.

John Smith is the smallest giant in the world. He's five foot ten.

WHAT NOT TO DO IN A HOLLYWOOD HORROR MOVIE

Do not, in any circumstances, go into the cellar, especially if the power has gone out.

Do not mess with anything that might open a portal to Hell.

If you find a town that looks deserted, there's probably a good reason for it. Stay away.

Beware of strangers carrying chainsaws, shovels, crucifixes, staple guns, hedge trimmers, beheaded dolls (especially if they look about 45 years old).

If electrical appliances start turning themselves on, move out.

If your kid is talking to you in Latin, or if you can't recognise in what language they speak to you at all, shoot them.

If you are fleeing from a monster, you will stumble and maybe fall at least twice (double this figure if you are a woman). Although it might appear that the monster is just shuffling along, it will still be able to catch up with you.

Do not read aloud old musty tomes that speak of demon summoning.

Never split up from the rest of the group and never walk backwards.

Ladies, remember that the monster will go for the woman with the biggest boobs. Hide your curves with shapeless tops and unattractive trousers.

Do not follow prints on the floor that look like drops of blood.

If you get offered a big house for a fraction of its selling price, there's probably some kind of morbid history attached to it. Don't buy it.

Be wary of any key that you find in the attic in one of your great-grandfather's old trunks, especially if it has weird lettering on it.

Never stand in, on, above, below, beside, or anywhere near a grave, tomb, crypt, mausoleum or other house of the dead.

THINGS TO PONDER

How do I set my laser printer to 'stun'?

How do signs reading 'Do not walk on the grass' ever get there?

If the black box flight recorder is never damaged during a plane crash, why isn't the whole aeroplane made out of the same stuff?

Why don't they just make mouse-flavoured cat food?

What's the speed of dark?

Why doesn't Tarzan have a beard?

Why can we never see baby pigeons?

How come wrong numbers are never busy?

Are part-time bandleaders semi-conductors?

Do jellyfish get gas from eating jellybeans?

If blind people wear dark glasses, why don't deaf people wear earmuffs?

Why is it that when you transport something by car, it's called a shipment, but when you transport something by ship, it's called cargo?

Why does your nose run and your feet smell?

Why do they sterilise the needles for lethal injections?

When you choke a Smurf, what colour does it turn?

What was the best thing before sliced bread?

What was Captain Hook's name before he lost his hand?

Is there such a thing as a not-free gift?

Chapter 13
Sport jokes

QUICK THINKING

Sir Alex Ferguson is on *Who Wants To Be A Millionaire?* and has reached the million-pound question. Chris Tarrant says, 'Right, Sir Alex; this is for one million pounds, and remember, you still have two lifelines left, so please take your time. Here's your question: What type of animal lives in a sett?

Is it,

a) a badger
b) a ferret
c) a mole or
d) a cuckoo?'

Fergie ponders for a while and says 'No, I'm sorry, Chris, I'm not too sure. I'll have to go 50-50.'

Chris says, 'OK, Computer; take away two wrong answers and leave the one right answer and one wrong answer.'

"Badger" and "cuckoo" are the two remaining choices.

Fergie has a long think, then scratches his head and says, 'No, Chris, I'm still not sure; I'm going to have to phone a friend.'

'So who are you going to call, Sir Alex?' says Chris.

'Hmmm...' ponders Fergie. 'I think I'll call David Beckham.'

So Tarrant phones David Beckham. 'David, this is Chris Tarrant from *Who Wants To Be A Millionaire*? I've got Sir Alex Ferguson here, and with your help he could win one million pounds. The next voice you hear will be Sir Alex's.'

'Hello, David', says Fergie. 'It's the boss here. What type of animal lives in a sett? Is it a badger or a cuckoo?'

'It's a badger, boss,' says Becks without hesitation.

'You sure, son?' says Fergie.

'Definitely, boss. One hundred percent. It's a badger. Definitely.'

'Right, Chris,' says Fergie, 'I'll go with David. The answer's a badger. Final answer.'

'Sir Alex,' says Chris, 'that's the correct answer. You've won one million pounds!'

Cue wild celebrations.

Next morning at training, Fergie calls Beckham across. 'Son, that was brilliant last night. I thought I might be taking a gamble giving you a call, but you played a blinder! But how the HECK did you know that a badger lives in a sett?'

'Oh, I didn't, boss,' replies Beckham, 'but everybody knows a cuckoo lives in a clock.'

DUMB AND DUMBER

Here is a written test given to would-be footballers. The time limit is three weeks. If the candidate cannot write, answers can be taped or drawn in coloured pencils.

Name: ______________________________

1. What language is spoken in Spain?

2. Give a dissertation on the growth of broccoli culture in ninth-century England OR give the first name of Charles Darwin.

3. Would you ask Celine Dion to:
   (a) build a bridge
   (b) sail the ocean
   (c) lead an army or
   (d) SING A SONG

4. What religion is the Pope? (check only one – beware, this is a trick question)
   (a) Jewish
   (b) CATHOLIC
   (c) Hindu
   (d) Polish
   (e) Agnostic

5. Metric conversion. How many feet is 0.0 metres?

6. What time is it when the big hand is on the 11 and the little hand is on the 6?

7. How many Deadly Sins are there? (approximately)

8. What are people in America's far north called?
   (a) Westerners
   (b) Southerners
   (c) Northerners

9. Spelling: spell Blair, Brown and Merton
   Blair: ________________
   Brown: ________________
   Merton: ________________

10. Six kings of England have been called George, the last one being George the Sixth. Name the previous five:

11. Where does rain come from?
    (a) a rain factory
    (b) Scotland
    (c) the Continent
    (d) THE SKY

12. Can you explain Sir Isaac Newton's law of gravitation?
    (a) Yes
    (b) No

13. What are bottle openers used for?

14. 'God Save the Queen' is the national anthem of what country?

15. Advanced maths: If you have three apples, how many apples do you have?

AVOID EXCITEMENT

A little boy is the subject of a bitter argument between mum and dad in court. Each of them wants him to live with them. The judge notices the boy's distraught face and beckons him to a private audience while he adjourns the court.

'I guess nobody actually thought of asking you what you'd like to do,' the judge says to him.

'No, they didn't,' the boy replies forlornly.

'You can tell me now. Would you like to be with your mum?'

'Nah: she's mad – she hits me all the time.'

'Oh: this wasn't mentioned anywhere in the case,' the judge notes with a frown. 'So you'd prefer to be with your dad then?'

'Nah, not really: he hits me even worse than my mum does.'

The judge is quite appalled by the little boy's situation.

'Well, is there anywhere you'd like to go? I mean, I'm the judge: I can make things happen.'

A ray of hope shines on the boy's face. 'I'd like to live with Watford Football Club.'

'Watford Football Club?' the judge exclaims. 'What on earth for?'

'Well, they never beat anyone.'

ALL OF A QUIVER

On an archery field, a guy is taking far too long to shoot. You are allowed a certain amount of time to aim, but this guy is really taking the piss. He's been there, his bow drawn, for two full minutes, ready to fire… only to stop, pull off and breathe before starting all over again. Everybody is waiting for him to finish so they can check their score. After the seventh attempt, one of his fellow archers has had enough: 'Come on, man. You're holding everyone up.'

'I know, but it's my wife there on the side. I want to make it the perfect shot.'

'Don't fool yourself,' the guy snorts. 'That's over 150 yards. You'll never get her from here.'

THE PERFECT CRIME

On a Monday evening, a guy tells his wife he's off to buy some cigarettes. When he's got his cigarettes, he looks at his watch and calculates that he's got enough time for a quick drink.

In the pub, savouring his cold beer, he is chatted up by a gorgeous young woman. She finds him witty and handsome and, after a few drinks, astonishingly sexy. Now, this is not something he's heard that often lately and he starts to be quite attracted to this lady and accepts her offer for a drink at her place. A few minutes later he finds himself wrapped up in a steamy embrace and they make love until late that night.

Coming out of a well-earned nap after sex, the guy looks at his watch again.

'Oh my God! Midnight! What will my wife say? I told her I was going to get some fags and here I am, in bed with another woman!' he realises with a start. He's got to do some quick thinking.

'Honey, I have to go,' he tells the beautiful creature sprawled naked and satisfied on the bed. 'Say: you don't happen to have some talcum powder, do you?'

'Mmm? Talcum powder? Sure: in the bathroom,' she answers dreamily.

A few minutes later he's out in the street, rushing back

home. His wife is waiting for him in the living room, sitting on the sofa, scowling darkly.

'Where have you been?' she asks in an ominous tone. 'I can't believe it took you six hours to get some cigarettes.'

'You're right, honey,' the guy says, thinking that telling the truth is his best option. 'I got the fags and then I went for a drink. There I met this woman and… well, she seduced me. I'm so sorry. I've been unfaithful to you; I've been having sex with someone else.'

The wife stands up from the sofa and approaches him with a very determined stride.

'Oh, yeah? Let me see your hands!' she orders him.

The husband turns his hands over with feigned reluctance.

'You bloody liar! Talcum powder! I knew it! You've been bowling again!'

TOPICALITY TIME

David Beckham goes to the pub.

'A pint, David?' the barman asks.

'No, a half and then I'm off.'

THE LORD GIVETH AND THE LORD TAKETH AWAY

A priest is off playing golf on a Sunday. When he woke up this morning the sun was shining, the air was crisp and he just couldn't let that pass: he's been wanting to play for ages. So he phones a friend of his, also a priest, and asks for a favour and here he is now, concentrating on his swing. The birds are singing, the air smells of pine and freshly-cut grass and an angel leans over to whisper in God's ear: 'He's deliberately lying to his flock! You can't let him get away with that!'

God hushes the angel and watches as the priest swings. The golf ball arcs across the sky in a perfect parabola, with majesty and grace, and lands on the green, 250 yards away, where it gently rolls towards the flag and finally plops into the hole.

'A 250-yard hole-in-one putt? You can't let him get away with it!' the angel gasps.

'And why not? Who's he gonna tell?' chuckles God.

PLAYING DIRTY

Harry is sitting on a bench playing idly with his tennis racquet. Along comes a stranger called Tom, who asks him if he wants to have a game. He agrees. They stroll to the reception desk and book a court half an hour from now.

They wait a whole hour: then Harry decides that's enough and he walks out to ask the players to hurry up.

Five minutes later he's back, his face pale and cold sweat pouring down his forehead.

'You won't believe it,' he says to Tom. 'the players on our court... one's my wife, the other's my mistress!'

'That's a bit awkward, hey?' Tom laughs. 'OK, I'll go and ask them to buzz off.'

Two minutes later, Tom is back, pale as a sheet.

'What's the matter?'

'Small world,' answers Tom.

WORTH THE PAIN

A group of women is playing golf. One of the women tees off and, to her horror, her ball heads towards the group of men ahead of them. Transfixed, she watches helplessly as one of the guys suddenly collapses, clutching his mid-section.

The guilty woman runs to the group of men and approaches the injured guy.

'Let me help. I'm a physiotherapist; I know what to do.'

'No, it's OK,' the man whines, still bent in two with his hands on his crotch.

'Don't be a baby. Honest, it's my job! I won't hurt you.'

The man lets himself be persuaded and soon, after the physiotherapist/terrible golfer has asked people to turn around, she takes the man's pants down and starts to gently massage his penis. After a few minutes, she asks the guy: 'Now, it wasn't that terrible, was it? How does that feel?'

'Oh, it feels great,' the guy replies. 'I still think my thumb's broken, though.'

FAIRWAY TO HEAVEN

A mechanic and a priest are off playing golf one day. The priest plays relatively well, while the mechanic is absolutely hopeless. He places himself as best he can, squints his eyes and swings. The ball arcs in the air and lands in a thicket.

'Oh, shit,' the mechanic swears. 'Missed.'

'Don't swear, my son,' the priest admonishes him and he's off delivering the perfect drive – again.

They walk to the next hole. The mechanic concentrates, bites his tongue, turns his shoulders… and hits the ball too hard. It lands in the sand.

'Ah, bollocks,' he swears. 'Missed again.'

'Do not swear, my son,' chides the priest. 'If you carry on swearing, you'll incur God's wrath.' This having been said, he hits the ball and it lands beautifully in the middle of the green.

After a few attempts, the mechanic has finally managed to put a ball on the green too and he's about to put it in the hole. Ever so carefully, he swings his club and the ball misses the hole by a good metre.

'Fucking shit!' he explodes. 'I hate golf! It's a fucking stupid game anyway.'

'I told you already, stop swearing! You put your soul in danger every time you proffer an obscenity and you will be punished.'

Just at this moment, the sky over them turns an ominous dark. The wind suddenly picks up and a gigantic bolt of lightning strikes the very spot where the priest is standing. The mechanic is hurled to the ground and when he stumbles back up, the priest is gone. All that is left is a golf club and a smoking cassock. A booming voice is heard coming from the heavens and says: 'Bollocks. Missed again.'

OCCUPATIONAL HAZARD

A caddy has been around the course today and has picked up a fair number of golf balls. He shares the load equally in his pockets and walks to the bus stop. At the door of the bus, he has to fumble in his pockets to find some change. In doing so, he gets all the balls from his left pocket into his right.

Finally, he pays the driver and goes to sit near an old lady. Unfortunately, all these balls in his right pocket make his sitting a bit uncomfortable and he keeps on squirming and fidgeting, trying to find a comfortable position.

'Is something the matter, dear?' the old lady next to him asks.

'Oh, it's nothing,' the caddy replies and then explains: 'Golf balls.'

'Oh, I see. Is that a bit like tennis elbow?' the old woman asks innocently.

CRUEL... BUT FAIR

What's 40 feet long and smells like urine?

Line-dancing at the nursing home.

A FIRST TIME FOR EVERYTHING

Three football fans go to the pub one day. They discuss the merits of their relative teams until closing time, then slowly head back home. On the way, they stumble upon the shape of naked woman lying in the middle of a dark alley. One of them decides to investigate and soon calls the others.

'She's dead,' he gasps.

'Dead? You're sure?'

He lifts the naked woman's hand and feels for a pulse. Nothing.

'Yes: dead. Tony – got your mobile on you? Good: phone the cops.'

While they wait for the police to arrive, the three chaps look at one another and wordlessly decide to cover the unfortunate lady.

One put his Arsenal woolly hat on her left breast, one puts his Manchester United woolly hat on her right breast and the last one puts his West Ham woolly hat on her genitals.

The cops don't take too long to arrive. The inspector interviews the three guys in turn and walks over to the victim to check for any external mark of abuse or rape. He inspects the breasts and then takes the West Ham hat off to inspect the dead woman's fanny. After a brief look, he puts the hat back on again. He takes a couple of steps back then, with a puzzled expression, lifts the hat again to have a closer look. He does this a couple more times and every time he looks more puzzled than before.

'What's the creep doing?' asks one of the football fans in a disgusted tone. 'He keeps on going for her fanny. The guy's sick.'

'Oh, it's nothing like that,' replies the policeman, who has overheard the comment. 'Only it's the first time I've seen something other than an asshole under a West Ham hat.'

YOU'RE A PAL

At 78, Raymond is still a very good golf player. His stance is perfect, his swing marvellous. He's got only one problem: he can't see very well any more. More often than not, he can't really see where his ball is going and it's starting to be a real problem. Irritated at having to ask for help, he nonetheless asks his old friend John if he wouldn't mind giving him a hand.

'I don't want any advice or anything,' Raymond warns gruffly. 'All I want is you to tell me where the ball goes, OK?'

John accepts and off they go one day, shuffling slowly in the morning air to the first hole.

Raymond peers ahead, manages to see the little flag way off in the distance and swings. The ball, as usual now, travels far too fast for him to see it.

'Can you see it?' he asks John.

'Oh yes, no problem. Beautiful shot,' John congratulates his friend.

Raymond waits a minute and then asks: 'Right. Now. Where is it?'

John is silent for a while, then replies: 'I forgot.'

GAMES PEOPLE PLAY

In an attempt to influence the members of the International Olympic Committee in their choice of venue for the games in 2008, the organisers of Liverpool's bid have already drawn up an itinerary and a schedule of events. A copy has been leaked and is reproduced below.

Opening ceremony:
The Olympic flame will be ignited by a petrol bomb thrown by a native wearing the traditional costume of boiler suit, baseball cap and balaclava. It will burn for the duration of the games in a large chip van placed on the roof of the stadium.

Events:
In previous Olympic Games, Liverpool's competitors have not been particularly successful. In order to redress the

balance, some of the events have been altered slightly to the advantage of local athletes.

100 metres: Sprint competitors will have to hold a video recorder and a microwave oven under each arm. On the sound of the starting pistol, a pit-bull terrier will be released from a cage 10 yards behind the athletes.

100 metres hurdles: As above but with added obstacles eg. car bonnets, hedges, garden fences, walls.

Hammer: Competitors in this event may choose the type of hammer they wish to use (claw, sledge etc.). The winner will be the one who can cause the most grievous bodily harm to members of the public within the time allowed.

Fencing: Entrants will be asked to dispose of as much stolen silver and jewellery as possible in five minutes. They will use baseball bats to fend off policemen armed with truncheons.

Shooting: A strong challenge is expected from the local men in this event. The first target will be a moving police van. In the second round, the competitors will aim at a post office clerk, a bank teller or a wages delivery guard.

Boxing: Entry to this event will be restricted to husband-and-wife teams and will take place on a Friday night. The husband will be given 15 pints of Tennent's while the wife will be asked to provide oral sex when he gets home. The bout will then commence.

Cycling time trials: Competitors will be asked to break into the University bike shed and take an expensive mountain bike owned by some mummy's boy from the country on his first trip away from home. Tools will be available to cut wire, locks and chain-link fences.

Cycling pursuit: As above, but the bike will be owned by a visiting member of the New Zealand rugby team who will witness the theft and take any action they deem appropriate.

Modern pentathlon: Amended to include mugging, breaking and entering, flashing, joyriding and arson.

Swimming: Competitors will be thrown off the Pier Head into the Mersey. The first three survivors back will decide the medals over a pint.

Men's 50km walk: Unfortunately, this will have to be cancelled as the police cannot guarantee the safety of anyone walking the streets of Liverpool at any time anyway.

The closing ceremony:
Entertainment will include formation rave dancing by the members of the Liverpool Health in the Community anti-drug campaign team, as well as synchronised brick-throwing. The Olympic flame will be extinguished by someone dropping an old washing machine on to it from the top floor of the block of flats next to the stadium. The stadium will then be boarded up before the local athletes break into it and remove all the copper piping and the central heating boiler.

ON THE SLIDE

Three teams are competing for the title of Olympic champion in ice skating: the Russian, the Italian and the British.

The Russian team perform admirably, without making any technical mistakes, although their performance is not very artistic, to say the least. The judges award the following marks: France 5.2, United States 5.3 and Ireland 6.0

The Italian couple are more flamboyant: great costumes, great rhythm and great choreography. Unfortunately, they don't have the technical mastery of their Russian counterparts and they do make a few mistakes: not much, but enough for their marks to be noted down as follows: France 5.4, United States 5.4 and Ireland 6.0

The next couple, however, are a disaster. Their attire isn't co-ordinated, they aren't in time with the music and the man even stumbles and nearly falls at the end of a triple salko. In brief, the routine is a mess and the marks reflect the poor quality of technical and artistic skills: France 4.8, United States 4.9 and Irish 6.0

The French and the American judges turn in surprise to their Irish colleague.

'How can you give this mess such a high score?' the French judge asks.

'Well, you have to remember something,' says the Irish judge in his defence, 'it's damn slippery out there.'

A HOLE NEW BALL GAME

A man is playing golf, badly. He keeps on getting lost and he doesn't know what hole he's supposed to play. He spots a woman playing ahead of him, so he resolves to swallow his pride and ask her for help.

'It's easy,' the woman player tells him. 'I am on the seventh hole and you're playing behind me, so you're on the sixth hole.'

The guy thanks her and carries on playing – badly.

Half an hour later he's lost again. He walks up to the same lady again and asks her for direction.

'I'm on the ninth hole and you're still one hole behind, which means you're on the eighth hole.'

The guy manages somehow not to disturb the lady again and finishes his round with a bad score, but at least he's completed the course.

Back at the clubhouse, he meets the woman again.

'Come on: let me buy you a drink,' he pleads. 'You've been so helpful and patient today, it's the least I can do.'

The woman accepts, and soon they're chatting away.

'So, tell me, what do you do?' asks the man.

'I can't tell you,' she replies. 'If I do, you'll laugh.'

'No, I won't, I promise.'

'Oh, yes, you will. Never mind. I work in sales. For Tampax.'

The guy stares at her and bursts out laughing.

'I told you you'd laugh,' the woman says, a bit offended.

'I'm not laughing at your job,' he replies, hiccupping with mirth. 'You see, I'm in sales too. I'm working for Preparation H. Looks like I'm still a hole behind you!'

NUTS ABOUT WINNING

An American wrestler is about to enter the ring. His opponent is a beast of a Russian guy, towering above him by a head and impressively muscular. The American coach takes his man aside and tells him to beware of the other guy's famous 'Pretzel Hold'.

'If ever he manages to pin you down, don't let him twist your left arm behind your back. He's got this Pretzel Hold trick and there's nothing you'll be able to do to get out of this position.'

The wrestler nods and, impatient to fight, jumps into the ring.

They grab one another, they grapple, they try to get one another off balance. What the Russian has in sheer force, the American counterbalances in flexibility and vivacity. They've battled for 15 minutes when the American slips. The Russian seizes this opportunity to grab him, heave him in the air and slam him back on to the floor of the ring. The American, dazed, realises that he's being pinned down, tries to escape, but soon the Russian has his left arm behind his back and here he is – held in the infamous Pretzel Hold. The American can't move a muscle. He's totally locked.

The crowd is delirious. They hail the Russian as the new champion as the judge approaches the American to count.

All of a sudden the American screams and literally jumps three feet into the air and lands on the Russian, knocking him cold.

It is the end of the match and the American coach, tears in his eyes, congratulates his most worthy student.

'Well done: well done, my son! I'm so proud of you,' he cries. 'When I saw you like that on the floor... you're the first one ever to escape his Pretzel Hold. How did you do it?'

'Well,' the guy replies, 'I was lying there and there wasn't a damn thing I could do. I was kind of like tied up and I couldn't move at all. All I could see was a tangle of body parts. Then this pair of balls got into my field of vision. The only thing I could move was my mouth and I thought, "What the hell: I've lost anyway; at least the bastard will remember me." I knew it was illegal, but I didn't care. So I bit these balls with all the strength I had. You saw what happened then: it's quite amazing how strong you get when you bite your own balls.'

A SLIPPERY SLOPE

Three guys have arrived at a ski lodge and want to book a room. There is only one room left, so they grudgingly agree to share the double bed for the night. The night passes and, in the morning, the man who slept on the left wakes up and says.

'I had the weirdest dream ever. I dreamed I was having a hand job.' To his surprise, the guy on the right says that he's had exactly the same dream.

'That's funny,' says the guy in the middle. 'I didn't have any weird dream like you guys: I dreamt I was skiing.'

AHA! CAUGHT YOU!

A woman asks her husband: 'If I were to die, would you marry again?'

'I don't know,' he replies. 'I suppose I'd be sad for a while and then, you know, life goes on. Yes, I might marry again.'

'Would you live together in the house?'

'We're paying quite a lot for this house and it's close to work. Yes, I'd probably live here with her.'

'And would you make love to her in our bed?'

'Honey, you have such strange questions! I mean, we just bought this bed. I guess I won't have that much money if you go so, yeah, I guess we'll sleep together in this bed. After all, it's my bed too.'

'And would she play with my set of golf clubs?'

'Oh, no: she's left-handed.'

BAD BEHAVIOUR

At half-time during a football match, the coach says to one of his young players: 'Do you understand what co-operation is? What a team is?'

The little boy nods in the affirmative.

'Do you understand that what matters is whether we win together as a team?'

The little boy nodded yes again.

'So,' the coach continued, 'when you have to go forward or move right, you do it. You don't argue and you don't insult the referee. Do you understand all that?'

Again the little boy nodded.

'Good,' said the coach, 'now go over there and explain it to your mother.'

MARVELS OF THE DEEP

A guy is diving for fun and has reached 15 metres when he sees another man, without any scuba gear on whatsoever. Puzzled, he gives the guy a wave and goes down an extra five metres. A minute later, the same guy's there, still with no scuba gear on.

Astonished, the diver picks up his slate and writes: 'How the hell do you manage to dive without scuba gear?'

The guy reads the plate, erases it and writes: 'I'm drowning, you moron!'

GIVE A DOG A BAD NAME

Two boys are playing football in Finsbury Park. Suddenly, one of them is viciously attacked by a pit-bull terrier. The other boy, reacting fast despite being pretty scared, sees a rusty length of pipe, takes it and whacks the dog on the head. The dog dies instantly and the boy rushes to his mate, lying on the floor clutching his leg and wailing.

Fortunately, a reporter has witnessed the scene. He tends to the light injuries of the boy who's been attacked and congratulates the hero.

'Arsenal fan saves friend,' he writes in his notebook.

'I'm not an Arsenal fan,' the boy says.

'Come on, boy: this is Finsbury Park. You've got to be a Gunner!'

'I'm not an Arsenal fan,' he repeats.

'OK, I see,' the reporter says. 'Who do you support then?'

'Man U.'

The reporter tears off the page in his notebook and instead writes: 'Man U fan murders beloved pet.'

HOOK, LINE AND SINKER

A man tells his wife after work: 'Honey, I have the opportunity to go fishing for a week in Scotland, all free, paid by the company as part of a staff development scheme.'

'That's pretty good,' the wife says.

'I kind of have to go, really,' the husband carries on. 'All my colleagues will be there, and my boss too. Ladder of success and Brownie points, you know…'

'Yes, this would be a great opportunity for you to get to know him better so that you can ask for a pay rise later on. Go for it.'

'Thanks, honey. Can you pack my bag? Put my blue pyjamas in.'

The wife dutifully packs his bag and the guy is off for a week's fishing.

When he comes back, his wife asks him if he's had a good time.

'Oh, it was great; but you forgot my blue pyjamas.'

'I didn't,' his wife replies sweetly. 'I put them in your tackle box.'

GAMESMANSHIP

This guy is at the bar above a pool club. He looks thoroughly dejected and is sinking beer after beer. A fellow-player comes to sit next to him and asks him what's up.

'Well, I had a bet with this guy,' he says glumly. 'He asked me for a game and he said I'd lose it, however many frames I did.'

'So?'

'So I asked how many frames he'd win by and he said he just needed two gotchas'.

'What on earth is a gotcha?'

'That's what I asked, but all he said was 'You'll see'.'

The guy buys him another beer and his friend continues.

'So here I was, carefully placing the balls, concentrating, and ready to put the red in the pocket, when suddenly he screams "Gotcha!"'

'Oh! I guess that was a bit of a surprise.'

'You can say that again. It threw me off totally. I missed the shot and nearly ripped the cloth of the table.'

'Still, that's only one shot. He said he needed two.'

'Yeah, well: have you got any idea how hard it is to play when you're expecting the next gotcha?'

I THINK I SPEAK FOR ALL OF US...

The ante-natal class is packed with pregnant women expecting soon. They are not alone: their husbands and partners are here too. There is an instructor today who's explaining that pregnant women need to remain fit. They need to do some exercises, such as pelvic floor strengthening and the like. The men are asked to perform the exercises with the women, and they do.

'Finally,' the instructor says, 'I would recommend you to be aware of your bodies. Being pregnant doesn't mean you can just spend all day on the sofa. You need to exercise. Be careful, of course, not to exercise too strenuously. Go walking: walking is very good for the heart. Guys, go for a walk with your partners and wives.'

A silence follows this statement and then one of the men asks timidly: 'Doctor, if we have to go on walks, is it OK for them to carry a golf bag?'

I'M ALL FOR CHARITY, BUT...

A pastor, a doctor and an engineer are playing golf and are waiting at a hole for the group ahead to finish. They are waiting and waiting, until it gets too much for the engineer, who goes to have a look and ask the players to hurry up a bit.

He comes back to his fellow-golfers with some sad news. 'It's a small group of blind firefighters,' he explains. 'They were out on a call last month when the building blew up. The club is letting them play out of charity.'

'How sad,' the priest says. 'We should say a prayer of thanks to the Lord for having spared them.'

'How sad indeed,' the doctor agreed. 'I have a friend: he's a renowned ophthalmologist. Maybe he can do something for them.'

'Yeah, well, why can't they play at night?' the engineer grumbles.

THE TEAM TO BEAT

Here is the new Italian line-up for the next European Cup.

Pinocchio

Libero

Vimto Memento Borneo Tango

Cheerio Subbuteo

Scenario Fellatio Portfolio

Substitutes: Placebo
Porno
Beano
Polio
Banjo
Brasso
Stereo (L)
Stereo (R)
Hydrochlorofluoro (GK)
Aristotle

FOOTBALL FOREVER

A Spurs fan dies one match day and goes to heaven in his Spurs shirt. Arriving at the top of the ethereal staircase, he knocks on the pearly gates – and out walks St Peter with an Arsenal scarf round his neck.

'I'm sorry mate,' says St Peter, 'No Spurs fans in Heaven.'

'What?' exclaims the man, astonished.

'You heard, no Spurs fans.'

'But, but… I've been a good man,' replies the Spurs supporter.

'Oh really,' says St Peter, 'What have you done then?'

'Well,' says the guy, 'A month before I died, I gave £10 to starving children in Africa.'

'Oh,' says St Peter, 'Anything else?'

'Well, two weeks before I died I also gave £10 to the homeless.'

'Hmmm. Anything else?'

'Yeah, on the way home yesterday I gave £10 to the Albanian orphans.'

'Okay,' says St Peter, 'You wait here a moment while I have a word with the boss.'

Ten minutes pass and St Peter returns, and looks the fan straight in the eye.

'I've had a word with God and he agrees with me,' he says, 'Here's your £30 back – now get lost!'

GOAL-DEN OLDIE

England are playing against Scotland in a friendly match. In the changing rooms Michael Owen stands up and says,

'You lot can go down the pub if you want. I'll play the game.' So the others go down the pub. While they're in the pub they check the score through teletext. With 15 minutes gone they check and see that Owen has put England one up. Now they keep doing this until they see that, in the 89th minute, Scotland have made it one all. So the players go back to the stadium where they find Owen crying in the changing rooms. 'What are you crying for?' asked Sven-Goran, 'One–one isn't bad.' 'You don't understand,' said Owen, 'I was sent off after 20 minutes!'

MICRO-WAVE GOODBYE

Beck's wife wants to buy a microwave. So she goes in to a shop and asks the salesman, 'How much for that microwave?' The salesman replies, 'I'm sorry, I can't sell you that.' So the next day she dyes her hair blond, puts on dark glasses, and goes in and asks the same question. The sales clerk answers, 'I'm sorry, I can't sell you that.' So the next day she puts on a woolly hat, shell suit, wig and false beard and goes and asks the same question. The salesclerk replies the same way. Posh then asks why on earth she's not allowed to buy the microwave, pointing at the object of her desire. The clerk says, 'That isn't a microwave it's a TV.'

CORNY

Sven-Goran Eriksson calls Beckham into his office.

'David', he says, 'I need to talk to you about your performance against Holland the other night, you were bloody hopeless, completely off form.'

'Sorry boss', says David. 'I've not been meself lately. I got problems at home, right.'

'Oh dear', says Sven. 'What's up? Posh and the kids OK?'

'Oh, they're fine right, it's just that something is really bugging me right and I'm losing sleep and everything right. I can't concentrate on me football and it's really messing me head up.'

'Whatever's the matter?' says Sven,

'Well boss, it's pretty serious. Victoria bought this jigsaw puzzle the other day right and...'

'A JIGSAW?' shouts Sven. 'You're playing like that because of a darned jigsaw?'

'Yeah boss, but you don't understand right, it's really doing me head in!' says David, 'It's really hard, it's this picture of a Tiger and it looks really easy on the box right and I'm sure I've got all the bits and everything but I just can't get it right and it's doing me head in and and...'

'David, David, David' says Sven, 'You really need to get a grip – and quick.'

'OK boss, but... It's this picture of a Tiger right and it looks really easy on the box right and I'm sure I got all the bits right and everything but can't do it and it's doing my head in and... and... it's a Tiger right and it looks easy but it's really hard right and er, it's a Tiger and everything, er... on the box... er... sorry boss.'

'OK, OK' says Sven, 'bring the jigsaw in and let's have a look shall we. It can't be that difficult'

'Thanks boss.' says David. So Becks brings in the jigsaw and takes it to Sven's office at the FA.

'Here it is boss', he says, showing Sven the picture on the box. 'Look boss, it's a Tiger right and it's a really good picture and everything but I just can't do it and it's really hard and its doing my head in and everything innit.'

Becks empties all the pieces from the box all over Sven's desk. Sven takes a glance at what's on the desk, looks up with his head in his hands and says to Beckham. 'Put the Frosties back in the box David.'